LIGHT ON THE SPIRITUAL PATH

Roy Eugene Davis is founder-director of Center for Spiritual Awareness, a New Era truth movement with an international outreach. He began his spiritual training with Paramahansa Yogananda in 1950. Mr. Davis is the editor-publisher of *Truth Journal* magazine, author of many inspirational books and a world-traveled teacher of meditation methods and how-to-live principles.

ROY EUGENE DAVIS
COLLECTED WRITINGS
Volume Three

LIGHT ON THE SPIRITUAL PATH

A Modern Treatment of the Bhagavad Gita
with Spiritual Commentary and a Clear
Explanation of the Esoteric Meaning
of this Classic Scripture of Yoga

CSA PRESS, *Publishers*
Lakemont, Georgia 30552

*Copyright © 1984
by Roy Eugene Davis*

This title is Volume Three of the Collected Writings Series. Contact the Publisher for a complete list of other available titles by the author: CSA Press, Post Office Box 7, Lakemont, Georgia 30552. CSA Press is the literature department of Center for Spiritual Awareness.

MANUFACTURED IN THE UNITED STATES OF AMERICA

Preface

My first exposure to the *Bhagavad Gita* came during my high school years, when I read a poetic rendition by Edwin Arnold titled *The Song Celestial*. Shortly thereafter I met my guru, Paramahansa Yogananda, in Los Angeles, California, and studied his spiritual commentaries on the *Gita*, which he had written over the years while teaching in America.

In the early nineteen-fifties, just shortly before his *mahasamadhi* (a yogi's conscious and intentional departure from the physical body), he had completed a more elaborate commentary, for publication in book form. As of this writing, however, his commentary has yet to be published. I visited him at his private retreat near Twenty-Nine Palms, California, a few weeks before his passing, and he told me that his *Gita* commentary had been completed, and that "a new scripture" had been born. He was satisfied that he had fulfilled his duty, relative to writing the commentary. We were in his living room, and he was resting on a large reclining chair, a gift to him from Mr. J.J. Lynn (whose monastic name was Rajarsi Janakananda) who was to succeed him as president of his organization.

Paramahansaji said, "A little while ago I was resting here, and meditating. I saw a golden light at the spiritual eye. I opened my eyes and saw the light against the wall, near the ceiling. As I watched it, Babaji, Lahiri and Sri Yukteswar appeared in the light and smiled their blessings. They wanted me to know they were pleased."

Mahavatar Babaji is the first in my guru line and remains on the planet in a subtle body. Lahiri Mahasaya is a disciple of this great avatar. Sri Yukteswar is a disciple of Lahiri and the guru of Paramahansa Yogananda. More details about these masters can be found in the biographical section of my book,

The Philosophy and Practice of Yoga, as well as in Yoganandaji's *Autobiography of a Yogi*.

There have been many excellent commentaries published on the *Gita* over the years. Shankara, that philosophical genius-seer of India who lived in the eighth century A.D., wrote a commentary which is considered important. Another, and more recent, commentary is the one by Sarvepalli Radhakrishnan. It is this latter text to which I refer persons interested in a deeper study. Radhakrishnan's version is the one I used when paraphrasing the verses.

This present edition is not intended as a scholarly work. I have rendered the translation freely, in modern English, to share the import and the meaning of the message for people in today's world. The value of the *Gita*, as with all great scriptures, is that it can be referred to time and time again, with the assurance that what one needs at the moment, in the way of guidance and instruction, will be provided.

Mahatma Gandhi, whose personal example and insistence upon practical application of spiritual principles has had such a constructive influence in the world, said this: "I find solace in the *Bhagavad Gita* that I miss even in the *Sermon on the Mount*. When disappointment stares me in the face and all alone I see not one ray of light, I go back to the *Bhagavad Gita*. I find a verse here and a verse there and I immediately begin to smile in the midst of overwhelming tragedies—and my life has been full of external tragedies—and if they have left no visible, no indelible scar on me, I owe it all to the teachings of the *Bhagavad Gita*."

It is my hope that this present offering will serve the reader well.

Roy Eugene Davis

Lakemont, Georgia
November 3, 1983

CONTENTS

Preface 5
Introductory Essay 9
The Confusion and Despair of the Soul 13
The Way of Knowledge 17
Freedom Through Right Action 33
Freedom Through True Knowledge 39
Freedom Through Perfect Renunciation 46
Liberation Through Meditation 53
God and Creation 61
The Pattern of Cosmic Unfoldment 67
Liberation Through Mystical Insight 72
True Oneness 78
Cosmic Awareness 81
Liberation Through Love 86
The Body, the Soul and the Faculty of
    Discrimination 89
Spirit and the Three Tendencies in Nature 93
The Mystical Tree of Life 97
The Positive and Negative Aspects of the Mind 100
The Three Kinds of Faith 103
The Supreme Renunciation 107

A Spiritual Examination of the Esoteric Meaning
    of the Bhagavad Gita 119

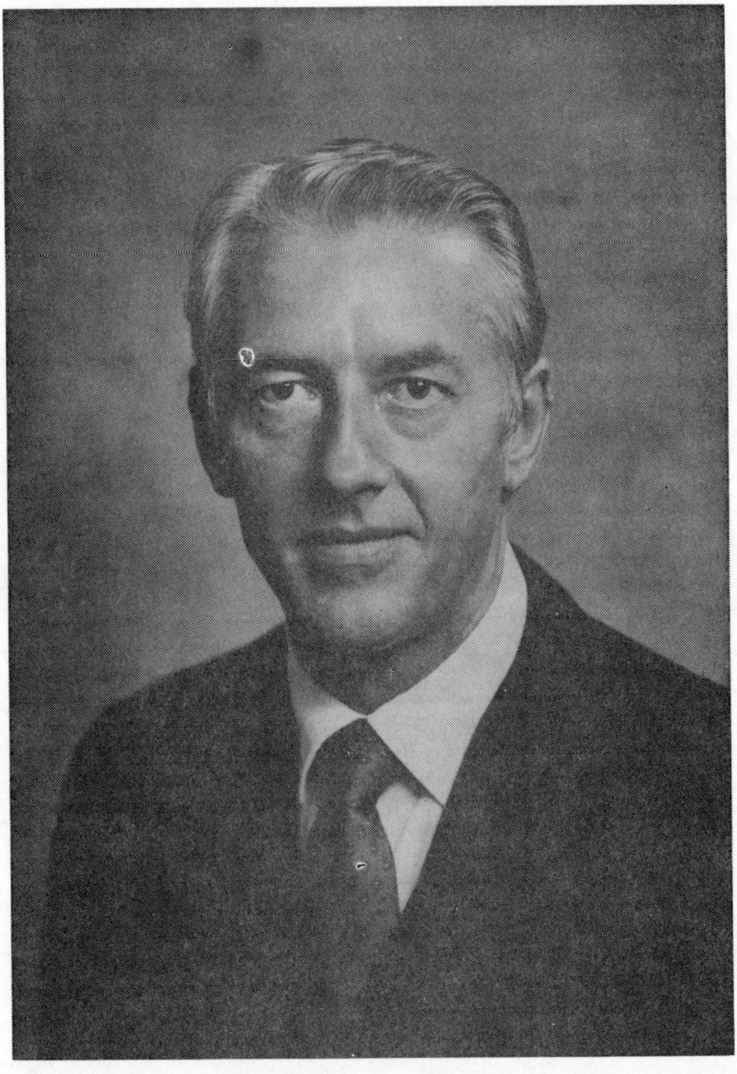

Introductory Essay

The title of this timeless spiritual treasure, the *Srimad Bhagavad Gita*, is translated from the Sanskrit language as "Glorious Celestial Holy Song." Written about the fifth century B.C., the text may have been somewhat revised over the centuries. Vyasa is said to be the compiler of the original text. The *Bhagavad Gita* is but a small portion of an epic poem, the *Mahabharata*: 220,000 lines divided into twelve books. The *Mahabharata* is a collection of poetry consisting of legendary philosophical material worked into and around a central heroic narrative which portrays the struggle between two families, one virtuous, the other with negative self-serving propensities. The purpose of the epic is to bring one to Truth consciousness and, therefore, it is said to be "sin-clearing and virtue-increasing."

The teachings of the *Vedas*, *Upanishads* and various philosophical traditions, including that of *Yoga*, are beautifully synthesized in the *Gita*. The text is, in fact, referred to as a *Yoga Shastra* or "scripture of Yoga." It is for all people, of all times and cultures, because its message is universal and touches both the human and the spiritual condition equally.

In the narrative, the scene is set on a battlefield. Arjuna is asked to fight his kinsmen and this he does not want to do. The outer picture is that of one facing worldly challenge, but the real import of the *Gita* is psychological and spiritual. There is a call to worldly duty, of course, but the clear message is one of aspiring unto knowledge and, finally, realization of God.

Arjuna represents a seeking soul, a true disciple on the spiritual path who must undergo transformation and purification if he is to awaken to the vision of Truth. Krishna represents the Transcendental Self of us all. Therefore, when Krishna speaks, we are to understand that God, the Higher True Self, is leading the soul back to the realization of Supreme Consciousness. The Self, the Real Nature, is Pure Consciousness. The "small self" is the soul, trapped by the temporary conviction that it is separate from God. It is all a drama, and an account of everyman's journey through space and time.

While Krishna is portrayed as the *avatara*, God having come into human form with full glory and power, the teaching is also that the *universal avatara* is already resident in, and as, every soul as the Supreme Self. The disciple begins with a doubt-filled mind, but is willing to learn. Eventually he awakens to realize that he, too, is as the Master: a full manifestation of the Divine Reality.

The message of the *Gita* is for the novice on the path as well as for the spiritually advanced. Here one finds advice of the most practical nature, as well as instruction leading to liberation of consciousness. Whether one be, by temperament, suited for the devotional approach to God-realization, or is inclined to knowledge, selfless service, or meditation, supportive guidance is here provided.

The way of righteousness is the way of ideal living, so that man's purpose on earth may be fulfilled and God's will might be surely done. Whenever the way of righteousness is neglected, the Divine Influence once again emerges on the world scene to encourage mankind to move steadily onward, to assure the maintenance of society and to illumine souls.

Three main themes are evident in the *Gita:* the way of selfless action or conscious attention to duty, the way of love and devotion which enables the devotee to surrender completely to God, and the way of wisdom, which is the way of error-free perception. Also emphasized is meditation, as a process which enables one to withdraw attention and life-force from externals in order to direct full concentration to the Transcendental Field of consciousness.

It is through meditation that one has the opportunity to directly experience the True Self, which is Pure Consciousness.

Introductory Essay

Meditation, as taught in the Yoga system, is a process by which one flows attention back to the source of Life within the body, and then transcends body as well as mental impressions. The True Self is already perfect. It is only when It becomes identified with mental activities and material processes that It somewhat loses Self-awareness. It may seem that we have challenges which have origins outside of ourselves; however, the truth is that we only have external challenge when we are not clear inside, when we are not settled in the conscious awareness of Who and What we really are.

The great contribution of Yoga is the science of *pranayama*, the procedure by which one is able to regulate nerve forces in the body, as well as more subtle currents of energy, in order to relax the body, clear the mental field and experience Pure Consciousness. All of the disciplines designed to assist in purification and transformation, including certain advanced meditation procedures, taken together comprise an intentional program known as Kriya Yoga. This was the emphasis taught by my guru, Paramahansa Yogananda, and is a most useful approach to Self-realization in our current New Era.

Among the meditation techniques included in the Kriya Yoga approach are *mantra*, contemplation and absorption in inner sound and light, and Kriya Yoga pranayama. Mantra enables one to have a focus for his attention during the early stages of meditation. Sound and light meditation enables the meditator to flow attention back to the Source, the field of Pure Consciousness. Kriya Yoga pranayama is a process by which one is able to circulate vital force through the spinal pathway, from the bottom to the brain, and to magnetize the spine and brain so that unused body forces are drawn into the *chakras* and brain centers. This process also neutralizes the decay processes of the body. Through Kriya Yoga practice the body is, in time, purified, and mental and emotional patterns which formerly restricted the soul are removed.

Man's perception of the outer world tends to keep him in bondage to it. When, however, through deep meditation, attention is turned within to the source of Life, an inner radiance

BHAGAVAD GITA

is perceived. One can then move through successive levels of mind to eventually experience That which is beyond mind.

There are influences through all of nature which are also influential in man's mind and body. These are three in number, and contribute to inertia, to activity, and to balance. In the *Gita*, Arjuna is counseled to rise free from all influences and to rest in the awareness of the Supreme Self. So long as one is dependent upon any material influence, there is the possibility of bondage through attachment. It is only when one transcends nature's influences that final liberation is experienced.

Chapter One

THE CONFUSION AND DESPAIR OF THE SOUL

The central characters of this narration are Arjuna and Krishna: the enquiring soul (every man) and the Divine Presence. We are all divine but many have forgotten this fact. Krishna, therefore, is the incarnation of the Supreme Spirit who stands as the unswerving example and gives clear advice every step of the way. The mystery of Krishna, the *avatar*, will be fully explained in the text.

The *Bhagavad Gita* is set forth as an account which took place centuries ago. Arjuna is faced with a common, though perhaps more obvious, problem. Because of inter-family rivalry and contention he finds himself placed at the head of an army which stands ready to do battle with his own kinsmen. Although he is obligated to play his allotted role in the defense of righteousness, he is heartsick because he must, in order to overcome the malicious intentions of the rival factions, enter into mortal combat and be the cause, so it seems to him, of the death of his own blood relatives. The *Gita* is not condoning war, as such. The battle is merely the incident used by the original author to tell the story of inner conflict and its eventual reconciliation, which is common to all individuals at one time or another. The physical confrontation to come is not as important to the narration as the psychological and spiritual transformation which is possible through inner readjustment and clear understanding.

Although the setting for the narration is the battlefield, referred to as the field of righteousness, the real enemies which must be faced and defeated are the psychological tendencies, addictions and inner patterns which prevent Self-actualization. The challenge and the ability to decide what is right in a special situation are unique to man. Hunger, sleep, desire for survival, and the urge to procreate are common to men and animals. A distinguishing characteristic is man's knowledge of what is right and what is wrong relative to a situation and to his purposes.

The world itself is a battleground for a moral struggle. The threats and challenges may differ according to individuals and occasions but life is ever a matter of making decisions and, according to how we make our decisions, so is our spiritual unfoldment determined. The reader will see almost at once that we are dealing, not with abstract philosophy, but with the challenge of moment-to-moment living. The message of the *Gita* is, therefore, a call to responsible action.

Even in the midst of the most impossible situation, there is always the possibility of our receiving divine guidance so that our spiritual growth is assured and the welfare of others is taken into consideration. We often come to an impasse when we reflect upon how our actions may influence others who do not share our understanding. Because of this we are, at times, driven to conform and to take the line of least resistance, or to allow ourselves to be put upon by others. We sometimes suffer at the hands of others rather than disagree with them because disagreement might upset them or hurt them emotionally.

After all, other people have their individual longings and their patterns to work out. How to live with people in the world and do right by them as well as ourselves, is the great question we must all face. If we are not careful, at this point, we might take the path of withdrawal and escapism rather than try to see through the appearances which surround us and understand them for what they are.

Spiritual teachers declare that the world about us is not as it seems at first examination. It should be looked upon as a game-situation in which many players are involved, most of them as blind participants. The goal of life, we are told, is Self-realization, and this is reached when we fully comprehend the nature of God and the cause and reason for the worlds. All true overcoming in this world is the result of spiritual growth. Without this understanding all human behavior is mechanistic and, in the long run, utterly devoid of reason. If we are here

The Confusion and Despair of the Soul

but for a few short years, to learn, to mate, to survive for a while and then die, to be no more, what is the purpose of it all? Why bother? Why not just adapt and go through the motions of living in a robot-like manner and have it done with?

To take the way of least resistance and arrive at the grave after a few decades of aimless living is not the purpose of our being in the world. To follow blindly the advice of those in authority and be a slave to conformity and tradition is to suppress our highest urges and deny personal growth. There must be a way to live so as to insure the stability of the social order and, at the same time, provide for the unfoldment of man's highest potentials; and there is.

Certain laws and traditions are useful to man's social well-being. There must be some guidelines if humanity is to go forward on an even course. Yet there must be room, within the pattern of the overall purpose, for the individual to function freely. To destroy institutions and disregard traditions without mankind as a whole having come to the place where it is divinely led, is a sure way to disaster. We observe certain outer rituals and rules of behavior in order to ensure group harmony, but this does not mean that, in time, rituals and rules cannot be modified to meet new and existing needs. Orderly transformation is required, rather than explosive revolution, and this, fortunately or unfortunately, usually takes some time to come about. It is to men and women of universal vision, endless patience, and purposeful action that the world is indebted.

A time of decision can be the turning point in a person's life. One can take the line of least resistance and fail to grow; he can give in to despondency and withdraw into his private psychological world and become uncaring, neurotic or even psychotic; or he can use his faculties of discrimination and intuition to make the correct decisions and follow through with intelligent and responsible action. The decision is man's alone to make. And how he makes it determines his future experience.

The time of decision is an opportunity for the soul to unfold. It is essential to spiritual progress. The feelings of aloneness, anxiety, fear, doubt and insecurity must be thrown off if man is to function successfully. There is a tendency for some people to feel that no one has ever faced their problems before; that somehow, due to their own miscalculations or due to the designs of a negative force, they have been singled out to be driven to their wit's end.

So, in the opening verse of this first chapter, Arjuna, the enquiring soul, faced with what seems to be an impossible problem, is confused and heartsick. But Krishna, the incarnation of Light and Wisdom, stands at his side and prepares to give wise counsel. Frequently, at times such as these, man is forced to contemplate the ultimate mysteries and open himself to an inflow of wisdom which will save him from himself and from the seemingly endless outside forces which threaten to engulf him completely.

It is taught in this philosophical treatise that God, the omnipresent Field of Consciousness, is really the larger True Self of every person. As waves on an ocean, so are we to the Infinite Ocean of God. Whenever a person is willing to turn to the Source for guidance, revelation will be given. Wisdom can surface from within, because all knowledge resides at the soul level, or it can be shared by one who is illumined. In the *Gita*, Krishna explains clearly the entire process of cosmic activity.

Chapter Two

THE WAY OF KNOWLEDGE

In this second chapter of the *Gita* we find Arjuna still in a state of confusion, compounded by extreme self-pity and self-justification. In order to release him from this condition, Krishna refers to the doctrine which declares that the soul is indestructible, appeals to his sense of honor and obligation, reveals God's purposes, and explains how constructive action is to be taken in the world if success is to be attained. Arjuna is still playing the role of the depressed and bewildered soul and utters, in the seventh verse:

> My very being is stricken with the weakness of pity. With my mind bewildered about my duty, I ask. Tell me, for certain, which is better, I am thy pupil; teach me as I seek refuge in your guidance. (7)

Realizing his inability to cope with outer situations with his feeble grasp of life's purpose, Arjuna makes a wise choice and turns to Krishna for instruction. Now he becomes a disciple, ready to listen to the wisdom of one who knows more than he. Arjuna knows, at this point, that his limited understanding is not sufficient as he contends with his difficulties, outward and inward, such as the differences in viewpoint of his friends and relatives, his doubts, fears, passions and desires. But even though he has turned to the Source for instruction, his mind is somewhat clouded and he is not totally receptive, as is evidenced by the following verses:

> I do not see what will drive away my sorrow which dulls my senses even if I should win the battle and emerge a material victor. I will not fight. (8,9)

Now Arjuna stops talking and becomes silent. Truth can only be perceived when the mind is stilled and intuition is awakened. In the narrative we are told that Krishna smiled, because he saw through the attempt at rationalization and wishful thinking of Arjuna. Krishna also knew what was going on within the disciple, and gently began to enlighten him with the following words:

> You grieve for those for whom you should not grieve, and yet you speak words of wisdom. Wise men do not grieve for the dead or for the living. Never was there a time when I was not, nor you, nor any man, nor will there ever be a time hereafter when we shall cease to be. As the soul passes in this body through childhood, youth and age, even so it takes on another body; the sage is not confused by this. Contacts with things of the world give rise to sensations of heat and cold, pleasure and pain. These come and go and do not last forever, so learn to endure them for a time while you seek higher wisdom. The man who is not troubled by these sensations, who remains unmoved during the course of temporary pain and pleasure, who is wise, makes himself receptive to the realization of eternal life. Know that the life that pervades all manifestation is indestructible and no one can alter or destroy it. The bodies of souls come to an end; therefore do your duty with an attitude of objectivity and renunciation. He who thinks he slays and he who thinks he is slain; both fail to perceive the real truth; no one eithers slays or is slain. (11-19)

Here is the cosmic view of the life process; souls incarnate time and time again in order to continue their unfoldment. However, they are not, in the real sense, born; nor do they die. When identified with the body, the soul assumes a viewpoint of being a body and experiences sensation in relationship to immediate perception and experience. We are advised neither to pursue pleasure for pleasure's sake, nor to overly react to temporary inconvenience. We are to understand the fleeting

The Way of Knowledge

nature of things and circumstances and strive to remain inwardly anchored in the realization of our unchanging reality. In this way we can transcend compulsive involvement with the world, as well as a frantic attempt to escape from it. Life in this world should be more than a pursuit of comfort or a retreat from discomfort. While putting our affairs in order so that we will not be bothered with unnecessary distractions, we should seek Self-realization while maintaining a lofty state of mind.

> He (the soul) is never born, nor does he die at any time, nor having once come to be will he again cease to be. He is, in truth, unborn, eternal, permanent and basically spiritual in nature. He is not slain when the body is slain. He who knows that he is indestructible and eternal, uncreated and unchanging, how can such a person slay anyone or cause anyone to slay? Just as a person casts off wornout garments and puts on others that are new, even so does the embodied soul cast off a tired body and take a new one. (20-22)

The soul was never born, but it had a beginning in relationship to the relative worlds. The soul is individualized Pure Consciousness. It is not separate from Pure Consciousness. The soul is a ray of Life and plays a role garbed in a body or vehicle at its particular level of expression. Wandering through time and space, the soul takes on bodies and discards them according to its conscious or unconscious needs.

Merely because Krishna is explaining to Arjuna the true nature of the soul is no reason for a person to feel that he has the right to go about depriving souls of their bodies by the seeming act of killing. Even though bodies expire, we should not be the intentional cause of such an act. We should wish all people well and leave their comings and goings, from body to body, to them, according to their own destiny and in line with God's will. Krishna tells Arjuna of the nature of the soul at this point in his instruction in order to elevate Arjuna's thoughts and give him a cosmic vision, so that he will be able to make future decisions in a better light.

"Murders, death in all its shapes, the capture and sacking of towns," wrote Plotinus, "all must be considered as so much stage-show, so many shifting scenes, the horror and outcry of a play; for here, too, in all the changing doom of life, it is not the true man, the inner soul that grieves and laments but merely the phantasm of the man, the outer man, playing his part on the boards of the world."

Whether we approve or disapprove, constant turmoil and subsequent change will go on in this world for a long time to come. We can work for eventual transformation of human consciousness, to be sure, but for the duration of the drama on the world stage we must hold fast to the inner truths and thereby establish a firm base from which to think, plan and act. In our modern society, whether we approve or not with the trend of the times is beside the point; we are involved. There is no possibility of dropping out or refusing to participate in some fashion. About the best we can do is to try to find our particular sphere of operation and do our best to bring about needed and useful changes within the framework of the social pattern. The central theme of the *Gita* is clear on one point: as long as we are involved in the human society we are involved with the behavior of society as a whole. Our taxes, our acceptance of governmental services, in fact every level of our human participation, is tied in with the consciousness of the country in which we live and the world we inhabit. There is no escape. We are compelled to communicate with others, and about all we can do is to follow the guidance of our highest intuitive leadings while we work for world solidarity and aspire towards a clearing of mass consciousness, so that the time will soon come when people as a whole will live in peace and be motivated by divine impulses.

When the physical body drops away due to accident, disease or old age, the soul is still able to function in a subtle body made up of mind, intelligence and life-force. The soul takes with it, from body to body, the memories, desires and feelings. Taking on a fresh physical body, it continues its spiritual journey.

The Way of Knowledge

> The soul, the true Self, is not harmed by weapons, burned by fire, made wet by water nor dried by wind. The soul cannot ever be harmed because it is eternal, all-pervading, unchanging and unmoving. It is the same forever. In the higher sense, the soul is unmanifest, unthinking and unchanging. Knowing this about the nature of the soul you should not grieve. (23-25)

Arjuna has been under the spell of the delusion which is common to millions of people. He did not know that the soul, being Spirit individualized, was immortal and changeless. Only when it identifies with one or a number of coverings or vehicles does the soul assume that it can be acted upon, be changed in some way or have beginning and end. On the spiritual path we are dedicated to the goal of consciously realizing our real, unchanging nature. And this is what our life is all about. We are not to become confused with various philosophies which declare that Self-realization is the result of learning through experience or the acquiring of much information. True Self-realization is experienced when we awaken from the mortal dream and remember our real nature as Pure Consciousness. Even many well-intentioned people, in their involved study of systems, teachings and philosophies, are missing the point and becoming more and more confused with life. One can be a truth student for dozens of incarnations and still be almost as badly misinformed and confused as the most hopeless materialist.

> Even if you think that the soul is perpetually born and perpetually dies, even then you should not grieve. For the one who is born death is certain and certain is birth for the one who has died. Therefore, for what is unavoidable, you should not grieve. Souls are unmanifest in their beginnings, manifest in their in-between states, and unmanifest at the end. So there is no cause for sorrow. (26-28)

When Crito asked Socrates, "In what way shall we bury you?" Socrates answered, "In any way you like, but first you must catch me, the real me. Be of good cheer, my dear Crito;

and say that you are burying my body only, and do with that whatever is usual and what you think best." For a person who knows that he survives the body, the form left behind is of small consequence. How different from the general attitude which prevails today of our reaction to the passing of a person, with our lamentations, our reverence for the body, and our elaborate and often costly provisions for its "eternal resting place!" Our behavior and speech often mirror our true convictions more obviously than our philosophical assertions.

Although birth and death must be considered for the person who is not yet awakened (from his point of view only), we are not condemned to the incarnational round forevermore. Eventually, through discrimination and intuitive perception, we awaken from the dream of mortality and cease to play the variety of roles imposed upon a person who is deluded.

In the very beginning souls became involved with manifestation. They became identified with the darkness, *maya*, the sense of illusion, the stuff of which creation is formed. Identifying with this fabric of nature and its components: time, space, motion, and light particles, the soul began its wanderings as in a dream. Through the process of right concentration and divine remembering the soul can become disentangled from the subtle medium of nature and recall its true reality as pure Life and Light.

> One person looks upon the Supreme Being as something marvelous, another speaks of Him likewise; still others hear of His marvelous nature; and even after hearing, no one whatsoever has known the nature of the Supreme. (29)

Even though the Supreme is considered to be great and all-encompassing by many people, no one (who is deluded) really knows the nature of God. Very few are willing to pay the price of complete self-surrender and self-emptying in order to be enlightened.

> Now, being reminded of your duty, you should not hesitate to act. There exists no greater opportunity for good than

The Way of Knowledge

to become creatively involved with pressing issues. (31)

Krishna advises Arjuna that now that he has been reminded of his duty he should set forth with a will and do what must be done, if he is to be victorious. Arjuna is further advised that for him to fail to attempt to fulfill his obligations would be wrong; that is, contrary to the laws of success and eventual well-being. Here we find practical advice for people at all stations in life. We learn that we are to do our duty, whatever it is, according to our ability and capacity, in the right spirit and with the correct attitude. In this way we further our own spiritual growth, as well as make a useful contribution to the unfolding world process.

Some people have mistakenly assumed that the ancient sages taught withdrawal from life and avoidance of responsibility. This is not true. What has been taught is that man can, empowered from on high, move through the world and be a force for good by fulfilling his obligations and assuming new responsibilities according to his capacity to execute them. When man performs his duties with the attitude that the Infinite Intelligence is working through him he does not incur any karma; that is, he does not create subconscious images or complications which will interfere with his future behavior.

This is the wisdom of the ancient seers which is now given to you. Listen now to this wisdom. If you can accept it by using the faculty of discrimination (intelligence) you can be relieved of the bondage of work. (39)

What Krishna is advising is that Arjuna let his intelligence govern his mind instead of letting the mind be impelled by the urges of the senses; then freedom is possible for him. One explanation of the symbolism of Arjuna's standing in a chariot preparing to go into battle, with five horses hitched to the chariot, is this: the soul (Arjuna) stands in the body (chariot) which is pulled (moved ahead) by the five senses. The faculty of discrimination is the driver of the chariot (senses) and functions through the mind. If the blind or deluded mind is free to work with the senses then chaos can possibly result. If, on the other hand, the faculty of discrimination (the intelligence) is illumined by the realization of God, then the guidance will be true and one's direction through life will be purposeful and without error. The sense of egotism (or the sense of separateness) must be relinquished before this can happen.

> On the true spiritual path, no effort is ever lost and no obstacle can long prevail; even a little effort to live the true spiritual life saves a person from great fear. On the spiritual path those who are firmly decided are single-pointed, but the thoughts of the undecided branch out in many directions and in endless variations. (40-41)

It is human nature to be confused and distracted. Not knowing our own mind, we are taken in by glamorous promises and impelled to action in order to gratify the desires and whims of the mind and body. Thus, life is often aimless and we come to the end of an incarnation with little or no progress being evidenced. However, we are advised, no effort is ever lost and no seeming obstacle can long prevail if we are determined. Eventually, our fears are vanquished and we begin to see through the mist with the eye of intuition, and the way becomes ever more clear with each succeeding step we take.

> The undiscerning people who rejoice in the letter of the scriptures, who contend that there is nothing else, whose nature is driven by desire and who are intent upon heaven, proclaim flowery words that result in rebirth as the fruit of actions, and prescribe various specialized rituals for the attainment of pleasure and power. (42-43)

Krishna here distinguishes true spiritual activity from ritualistic piety or self-serving (religious practices). In times past, as well as today, people have often prayed, fasted for religious reasons, and outwardly observed all of the rules enjoined by scripture in order to acquire some personal merit or gain. All of the talk of eventual heaven, hair-splitting dis-

The Way of Knowledge

cussions over scriptures (as well as blind adherence to them), high-sounding talk about cause and effect; all these are a waste of time. Likewise, are magical practices used by people to control the elements and manipulate others. The way to freedom is to give up vanity and yield to the inner Light so that It can do what It wills through, and as, us.

An explanation of the characteristics of nature is to be found in the scriptures; become free of these characteristics and tendencies of nature; be free from dualities, be firmly fixed in purity, not caring for acquisition and preservation, and be Self-realized. (45)

There are three obvious tendencies which run through all of nature: the tendency toward enlightenment, the tendency which causes man to be restless and remain involved in action, and the tendency which moves man toward inertia and causes him to be dull and lazy. These are referred to, in brief, as the elevating, activating and deadening tendencies. All people are influenced, to a great extent, by one or a combination of these tendencies or urges in nature. When influenced by the urge toward inertia, a person is indolent and dull. When influenced by the activating tendency, one is unsettled and engaged in activities. When influenced by the elevating tendency, a person aspires to the highest and best of which he is capable. The elevating current in nature draws creation back to the original condition of rest. The outflowing current, the cause of inertia, carries energy into manifestation at the time of creation. The activating current is the result of tension between the positive and negative poles.

Krishna suggests to Arjuna that he remove himself from any involvement with these tendencies in nature if he wants to attain Self-realization. To struggle with (or give in to) the tendency toward inertia, what men refer to as an evil force, causes spiritual blindness. To cooperate with the activating tendency is to be forever on the move, often without purpose. To strive to harmonize with the elevating tendency is better, but to become aware of the true Self and function from that awareness is best.

Even advanced metaphysical students who are forever affirming and visualizing "goodness, health and prosperity," have missed the point. Such effort is a clear indication that they have not yet realized the truth: that they are, as souls, already in possession of the very things that they are trying to obtain.

> As is the use of a pond, in a place flooded with water, so is the use of the scriptures for a Self-realized person. (46)

A person who stands in the clear recognition of the truth about Life, and who knows who he is, does not have to study anymore nor engage himself in useless action. A Self-realized person will seem to others to be good, but he does not concern his mind with trying to be good. He is conscious of being God in action.

> You have a right to action only and never to the results of action; let not results of action be your motive; neither let there be any attachment to inaction. Firmly established in the realization of your true nature, do the work at hand, giving up attachment to it, and have an even mind in times of outer success or failure, for evenness of mind is a way to peace and divine knowledge. Action alone is inferior to the discipline of intelligence. Those who work for results alone are to be pitied. One who has realized his true nature casts away both good and evil (thoughts and actions). Therefore, strive for Self-knowledge. Self-knowledge then remains, even in action. (47-50)

Here is an important and helpful point. When we do our work, regardless of what it is, if we think of fame or income or even of personal satisfaction, our goal is not a spiritual one. The majority of the people in an average society work for a living or work in order to gain the approval of others. No one can deny that compensation and recognition contribute greatly to our emotional well-being. But if we are working merely for income or for any satisfaction which might come as a result, we often perform useless actions. What we do could as well be done by a senseless person or by a machine. The question is this—what are we contributing to society?

Something else is involved here: if we are forever striving for results, looking for effects, we are chained to the cycle of action and reaction, the law of cause and effect. On the other hand, when we learn to function with an attitude of, "Not I, but Life, flows through me and does the work," then we are stepping free from compulsive involvement with our actions. A person who is in his right place and performs with the proper attitude has risen above the level where he sees good versus evil. He is rid of selfishness and is, therefore, incapable of harmful thoughts or actions.

> Wise people who have experienced enlightenment and who have renounced the results of actions and who have become freed from the ties of birth reach the state of joy and freedom. (51)

It is taught that a person who is concerned with causes and effects, when he leaves this realm, moves to an astral sphere peopled with others who share a similar state of consciousness; that is, with ordinary self-centered people. Those who pursue enlightenment, upon leaving the body, go to a more celestial realm with nearly enlightened souls. But the true selfless person experiences liberation and transcends all identification with the tendencies in nature.

> When your intelligence has crossed the confused maze of delusion, then you shall be indifferent to what has been heard and what is yet to be heard. When your intelligence, which is bewildered by conflicting scriptural information, is stable and unshaken in the realization of oneness (samadhi) then you shall attain insight. (53)

As a person who lacks the ability to discriminate ponders

various scriptures and metaphysical-occult book sources which are put forward by various schools of thought to support their theories, the mind is confused. When a person becomes enlightened, he understands the truth in scripture and intuitively knows that he, himself, could very well have written it. He can also discern the errors which have crept in over the centuries as the result of the meddling of scholars and self-serving religious teachers.

The main question for the average person is not what to do, for a man can only do what feels right to him according to his present ability and understanding. The important issue is how he works and what his attitude is while he is working.

Arjuna asks:

What is the description of a man who is firmly established in spiritual wisdom and whose being is steadfast in the realization of his immortal nature? How should such a man behave? (54)

Krishna answers:

When a man puts away the desires of his mind and when his Spirit, his inner nature, is content in Itself, then he is referred to as one who is stable in intelligence. He whose mind is untroubled in the midst of sorrows and is free from compulsive desire when surrounded by pleasures, he from whom passion, fear and rage have passed away, he is called a sage of settled intelligence. He who is without affection, who does not rejoice or despair as (so-called) good or evil come his way, his intelligence is firmly set in wisdom. He who draws his senses away from temptations as a turtle draws in his limbs (into the shell), his intelligence is firmly set in wisdom. Temptations cease for the embodied soul who abstains from them but the urge for sensual experience remains. Even this urge dissolves when the Supreme Vision is experienced. Even though a man may strive continuously for perfection and be extremely discerning, his impetuous senses will often carry off his mind by force. Having

The Way of Knowledge

brought all his senses under control, he should remain firm in the practice of yoga (meditation and contemplation) with all of his attention flowing to the real Source; for he, whose senses are under control, his intelligence is firmly set. (54-61)

Ideally, a general pattern should emerge in people's lives; they should, if they are fortunate and spiritually oriented, receive some spiritual training early in life, enter into the adult world of raising a family and being involved in the social fabric, begin to withdraw in late middle age, and spend their final years absorbed in study and meditation. This was the planned pattern of those who observed the Vedic traditions centuries ago. Unfortunately, in modern times the initial years of spiritual training are frequently passed over. What religious instruction received by all too many young people today is the result of their either being indoctrinated into the customs of their families, or exposed by chance to an orthodox religious teaching because it is considered by the parents that any religious instruction is better than none. Others, for better or worse, receive no religious or philosophical instruction at all.

In the ideal sequence of events, a person would retire from active participation in society and meditate during the latter years of his earth incarnation. Perhaps he would even be available for consultation to those who were desirous of enlightened advice. It is usually easier for a person to retire from social involvement after he has had experience in the world for a number of years. He has then lived his life and his curiosity is satisfied. He has also had an opportunity to work out some of his desires and urges, as well as to pay his debt to society. It is rare for a young person to succeed as a recluse because, usually, he is merely escaping from life. And, unless he has some worthwhile creative work to occupy his attention, he becomes an idle daydreamer or simply becomes complacent, useful neither to himself or to anyone else.

Even while we are playing our role to the best of our ability in this world, we can also strive to maintain the proper point of view and let our intelligence be illumined from on high. In this way, there is a feed-down of Divine Power which works Its way into the affairs of men. The secret of liberation is bound up in our ability to know that we are, as individualized souls, expressions of the Divine. It is not enough for us just to abstain from negative actions or irresponsible involvement. We can control our actions, but still the yearning to give in to temptation may remain in the subconscious, eating away, working at our vitals until we either break down or begin to manifest psychosomatic ailments. We are not merely to abstain from destructive behavior patterns; we are to remove from the consciousness any desire to be destructive or troublesome.

For a person who is vital and sensitive, it is not sufficient to try to be guided by a list of "thou shalt nots." Direction of attention is more useful. If we discipline ourselves to engage in positive thinking and positive action there will be little time left for idle thoughts. Eventually the inner Light begins to shine and human consciousness is purified and transformed.

Self-discipline is not a matter of intelligence only. Many intelligent people are at the mercy of their urges and tendencies. Even when the spirit is willing the flesh is often weak. What is needed is an exercise of the will and emotions. Proper direction of attention is important in the process. This is made easier as the result of our contemplation of the Infinite and as a result of our association with wise and enlightened people, either in person or through the reading and study of their written words. In this way we become attuned with their level of consciousness and soon begin to function in a similar fashion.

> When a man dwells in his mind on the sources of outside pleasure, attachment to them is produced. From attachment springs desire and from desire comes anger (if the desire is thwarted). From anger rises bewilderment, from bewilderment a loss of memory, from loss of memory the destruction of intelligence, and from the destruction of intelligence he perishes. But a man of disciplined mind, who moves in the world with the senses under control and free from attachment and aversion, he attains purity of

The Way of Knowledge

> spirit. And in that purity of spirit, there is produced for him an end of all sorrow; the intelligence of a man of pure spirit is soon established in the unshakable peace of the soul. For the uncontrolled, there is no intelligence; nor for the uncontrolled is there the power of concentration and for him without concentration, there is no peace and for the unpeaceful, how can there be happiness? When the mind runs after the roving senses, it carries away the understanding, even as a wind carries away a ship on the water. Therefore, he whose senses are withdrawn (from the objects of the senses), his intelligence is firmly set. (62-68)

Strong desires, we are told (and we inwardly know), can be as compelling as powerful external forces. They may literally lift us to the heights of self-discovery or they may cause us to abandon everything and be thrown into pain and disgrace. Who has not, at one time or another, felt the urge to give up everything for which he has worked, in order to possess the object of desire? Of course, no one ever perishes. However, spiritual perception can be clouded and a person can lose his way in life for a duration.

We should not hate ourselves or our urges, but we should learn to handle our urges and feelings. Through proper regulation of our strong drives we can accomplish many worthwhile things in the world. We can harness the mind and the emotions and, by careful planning and energetic work, become a force for good in society and thus transmute urges which otherwise cause us to wander without purpose and be the cause of self-recrimination and guilt.

One who is anchored in God covets nothing, is jealous of no one. He has no uncontrollable desires and makes no demands upon God or nature.

> What is night for all beings is the time of waking for the disciplined soul; what is the time of waking for beings is night for the sage who sees (who has clear vision). (69)

While people as a whole are striving for external things, the disciplined soul is working for Self-realization. Those who strive outwardly only are asleep; for them it is night. Compared to the disciplined soul who is working for freedom, the sage is wide awake; to the latter, even the seeking soul, though rightly resolved, is still asleep.

> He unto whom all desires enter as water enters into the sea, which though ever being filled is ever motionless, attains to peace, and not he who clings to desires. He who abandons all desires and acts free from longing, without any sense of possessiveness or egotism, he attains to peace. This is the divine state; having attained thereto, one is never again bewildered; fixed in that state at the hour of passing from the body one can attain to the bliss of the Supreme.
> (70-72)

The sage is unmoved regardless of the stream of impressions which flow through his mind and being. He has nothing in him of a gross nature with which such impressions can identify. When we leave this realm we do not have to look forward to various astral experiences, nor to the prospect of returning to this earth. If we are fully enlightened and we have cut off every tie with the world, then we experience transcendence. We can move directly into the Light. We do not have to grow into the Light.

Wisdom is said to be the supreme means of liberation. But, while we are here, we are compelled to perform some useful service as an outlet for our energies and as a means of neutralizing destructive and non-useful tendencies. Even while engaged in service to mankind for the good of the world, we attain liberation of consciousness when we are anchored in God.

Chapter Three

FREEDOM THROUGH RIGHT ACTION

Arjuna has drawn the wrong conclusion about activity in this world and has assumed that Krishna believes that knowledge without any action at all is better than work. This is clear from his opening question:

> If you say that the path of understanding is better than that of action, why then do you urge me to get involved in this battle which lies ahead? (1)

Arjuna's argument is this: if the way to attain wisdom is best, then why be involved in action at all since action, to obtain insight, seems to be irrelevant? Krishna has not intentionally tried to confuse Arjuna and so he continues, with gentle patience, to explain his philosophy:

> Arjuna, in this world a twofold way of life has been taught by me from times past (through Krishna and other embodiments of God), the path of knowledge for men of contemplation and the path of works for men of action. Not by abstaining from action does a man obtain freedom from it; nor by mere renunciation does he attain perfection. For no one can remain even for a moment without some kind of work; everyone is made to act by the impulses born of human nature. He who restrains his organs of action but continues in his mind to brood over the objects of the senses, whose nature is deluded, is said to be a hypocrite and a man of false conduct. But he who controls the senses by the mind and without attachment engages himself in useful work, he is honest and superior in his conduct. (3-7)

Krishna, as all true teachers do, recognizes that some are naturally indrawn and can pursue the contemplative path more easily. Likewise, there are those whose attention flows outward more strongly, and they crave involvement and activity. However, most people have both characteristics in their nature. They crave communication and involvement with the external world and they also desire the cultivation of the inner life. Both the way of complete renunciation and contemplation and the way of selfless action in the world are of equal value; the end is the same. An enlightened person works as an example to others, for the maintenance of the social order and to give vent to the energies which crave release and direction. The ideal is for a person to work, but without personal desire or selfish motivation, if it is at all possible. The tendencies in our nature, the weight of karma (subconscious impressions), and the necessity of providing for the body impel most people to do something in the world.

> Do the work set before you, for this kind of action is better than inaction; even your body cannot be maintained without some form of action being taken. But, work which is not done in the spirit of renunciation is binding; therefore, work in the spirit of renunciation and become free from all attachment. Know that the origin of karma (cause and effect) is in Divine Consciousness. Therefore, the Divine Consciousness is in and through all useful work. (8, 9 and 15)

The question is often asked, "As long as a person remains involved in action, how can he ever hope to be free of the consequent results of action?" The answer is: if we perform selfless action, working for the good of the world according to our capacities to serve, we perform non-binding action. Karma is then not accumulated. But this is very subtle; we must not work for praise or cease to work if blamed, and we must not be motivated by any internal or external urge, save from the highest consciousness. In the very beginning an urge in Divine Consciousness caused energy to flow out to manifest as the world process. This initial urge has resulted in everything else that has taken place in creation on all levels; therefore, the Divine is very much at work in the world. We are asked to participate in the Divine Plan if we are to know freedom.

> He who does not, in this world, help to turn the wheel which has been set in motion (from the beginning) is evil in his nature, sensual in his enjoyments, and he lives in vain. But the man whose enjoyment is in soul consciousness alone, who is in this wise content and satisfied, for him there exists no work that needs to be done. Similarly, in this world he has no interest whatever to gain by the actions he has done and none to gain by the actions he has not yet performed. Therefore, without attachment, perform always the work that is before you, for man attains to the highest by doing work without attachment. (16-19)

The individual and the cosmos depend upon each other, in the relative sense; there is a mutual interdependence. Therefore, a person who works for himself only, works in vain. We are not to work in order to please God, whatever our concept of God might be; we are to work properly so that we might become conscious that we are part of a grand and glorious cosmic process. A person who is Self-realized is not motivated from the subconscious level, nor from the unconscious level, nor from a sense of social obligation. He has a higher allegiance. We are not to expect blessings as a result of past actions, nor are we to work for any possible future blessings. We are to find freedom in the moment, as a result of working with the right attitude. The ideal attitude is, "I of myself can do nothing. The Father within he doeth the works." Working in the proper spirit, the mind is purified and destructive and non-useful patterns are neutralized.

> It was by selfless work that Janaka (a king who lived in India centuries ago) and others (like him) attained perfection. You should work also with a view to maintaining the world. Whatever a great man does, the same is done by

others who look to him as the example. Whatever standard he sets, the world emulates. There is not, for me, any work in the three worlds (physical, astral or causal) which has to be done, nor anything to be obtained which has not been obtained; yet I am engaged in action. For if I did not engage in ceaseless work, men on all levels of society might follow my example and the worlds would fall to ruin, and I would be responsible for the resulting disorder and destruction. (20-24)

The concept of the interconnectedness of society is deep in this philosophy. If the common life is to be decent and orderly, the world must work harmoniously in all its parts, from the subtle to the gross, through the enlightened and unenlightened alike. The aim of religion, in the highest sense, is to spiritualize society and establish brotherhood on earth. Some people, weary of the world, desire to forsake it. Active people tend to think of saving civilization and of creating a utopian condition. Wise men think of heaven and their vision of heaven externalized on the planet for the good of all. Enlightened leaders are the ones who set the example and inspire the masses; therefore, they must do what is right so that others can follow them. The redemption of souls and the transformation of human consciousness are the result of the inspired conduct of those who have caught the cosmic vision and who play out their role in full view of mankind.

St. Thomas wrote, "As the production of a thing into existence depends upon the will of God, so likewise it depends on His will that things should be preserved; hence if He took away His action from them, all things would be reduced to nothing." It is, according to the mystics, a spiritual crime to weaken the faith or unsettle the mind of a person in the world who is doing the best he can to survive and live up to the highest and best of which he is presently capable. Whatever we do for others we should do with love and reverence. We must take them from where they are to where they can go, according to their capacity to learn.

It is better to fulfill one's own law of life, even though imperfectly carried out, than to try to fulfill the life pattern of another and succeed in the attempt. (35)

Krishna is here saying that it is better for a person to work out his personal destiny according to his needs, urges, abilities and capacities, even if he is not completely successful in this incarnation, than for him to try to pattern himself after someone else's ideals and emulate him to the letter. By working with our own patterns, we learn our own lessons, accomplish our own overcoming and attain, eventually, liberation of consciousness. An outer life of success with an inner life that is hollow and barren is a waste as far as spiritual progress is concerned.

Arjuna speaks:

What impels man to commit sin, as if by force, against his own will? (36)

Krishna answers:

Craving and uncontrolled emotion, born of passion, is the only enemy here. As fire is covered by smoke, as a mirror by dust, as an embryo is enveloped by the womb, so is the covering of passion. The senses, the mind and the intelligence are veiled by passion and the soul is deluded. Therefore, control the senses and slay this destroyer of wisdom and discrimination. The senses, they say, are great; greater than the senses is the mind, greater than the mind is the intelligence, but greater than the intelligence is the soul nature. Thus, knowing this which is beyond intelligence, steadying the human nature by soul-control, slay the enemy of unreasoned desire. (37-43)

Sometimes, to justify behavior, we claim that we are forced, against our will, to commit wrong acts; that is, acts which complicate our lives or the lives of others. But if we are honest we must admit that we inwardly agreed, on some level of our being, to do the thing we did, for whatever reason we claim. Really, the reason we misbehave is that our intelligence, mind and senses are under the control of a strong urge, under control of passion, the desire to express, sometimes in a way which is not for the highest good of ourselves or others. And many people are, of course, fully conscious of what motivates them, but they have deadened their feelings and nothing is too wrong as long as their ends are served. Spinoza explained, as follows:

"For the things which men, to judge by their actions, deem the highest good are Riches, Fame and Sensual Pleasures. Of these the last is followed by satiety and repentance, the other two are never satisfied; the more we have, the more we want; while the love of fame compels us to order our lives by the opinions of others. But, if a thing is not loved, no quarrels will arise concerning it, no sadness will be felt if it perishes, no envy if another has it, in short, no disturbances of the mind. But the love of a thing eternal and infinite fills the mind wholly with joy, and is unmingled with sadness. Therefore, it is greatly to be desired and to be sought with all our strength."

Enlightenment teachers declare that certain fundamental social crimes are: appropriating that which belongs to another without their permission, class privilege, race discrimination or national egotism, for these involve pain to others. A consciousness must be cleared stage by stage; the more it is cleared the more free we are in a true spiritual sense.

In this chapter the message is clear: that since the Infinite caused the worlds to be, it is best for us to try to let the Infinite work Its will through, and as, us rather than for us to try to do God's will for God, without knowing how to do it.

Chapter Four

FREEDOM THROUGH TRUE KNOWLEDGE

I proclaimed this imperishable Yoga (this way to Self-realization) to ancient wise men and makers of the laws by which men are governed. They handed it down from one to another, through a line of royal sages, until this truth was lost to the world through a long lapse of time. This same ancient science has been today declared to you by me, for you are my disciple and friend and this is the supreme secret. (1-3)

Krishna explains that the Spirit of God (His true consciousness) revealed this science of soul-discovery to the ancient wise men and those who made the laws by which people are governed and their actions regulated. Furthermore, this information was passed down the line until, during the Dark Ages, it was misunderstood and lost from the world. Every 24,000 years (in 12,000 years ascending and 12,000 years descending) the consciousness of man is cleared or darkened; because of this we have Golden Ages and we have Dark Ages, with various shadings of enlightenment or delusion in between. When truth is lost from the minds of men, new teachers then come forward to light the flame of faith once more, and to show mankind the way to spiritual freedom.

Great teachers never claim to be original; they merely restate the great truths. This is the *Sanatana Dharma*, the Eternal Religion. Augustine called it the "wisdom that was not made; but is at this present, as it has ever been and so shall ever be."

Arjuna is clearly confused and asks:

You were born after those ancient teachers and lawmakers.

How am I to understand that you declared this truth to them? (4)

Krishna responds:

I have had many embodiments and so have you; all of them I remember but yours, you do not. Though I am, in a spiritual sense, unborn, and my true Self is imperishable, though I am (in a cosmic sense) the controller of all creatures; establishing myself in my own nature, I come into manifest form through my own magical power. Whenever there is a decline of righteousness and a rise of unrighteousness, then I send forth myself as a man among men. For the protection of the good, for the destruction of the wicked, and for the establishment of righteousness, I come into expression from age to age. (5-8)

This is the mystery of the *avatar*: God coming into the world in the form of man to redeem souls. Buddha, for instance, claimed to be the teacher of many enlightened souls of ages past. Jesus the Christ frequently asserted his relationship with his Heavenly Father. Mahavatar Babaji, the first in my own line of gurus, said that he initiated Swami Shankara many centuries ago, even though he (Babaji) is presently embodied on the earth plane, in his subtle form.

An avatar, one who is completely Self-realized, identifies himself as the Supreme Spirit. To such a one, the taking on and the leaving off of bodies is a matter of small consequence, and he has clear recall of all past actions. He knows all the roles he has played, while the average person forgets past embodiments with each succeeding incarnation. Avatars are concerned with man's progress over the centuries and whenever the mass consciousness becomes dark, one or a number of these perfected beings will come into the world to set the example, restate the changeless truths and clear darkness from the planet.

A free soul can, if he so desires, *will* to take on a body; he then identifies with world consciousness and comes on the scene. As the worlds were formed as a result of Cosmic Will,

Freedom Through True Knowledge

so a physical body is taken on by a liberated soul in a similar manner. Whatever such a soul does while on earth in no way influences him, and he incurs no karma whatever. His reason for being here is to do only the will of God. In time, Reality will eradicate seeming error and spiritual blindness will cease for all men.

Some individual souls have played the role of spiritual teachers in many cultures throughout the centuries. They are conscious of *living forever* with or without the same body. In a higher sense, Pure Consciousness is the *universal avatar* and functions through all individualizations of Itself. When the individualized soul begins to see beyond its sense of individualization it can acknowledge: "I am the Christ; I am the Buddha; I am the Most Ancient One; I am the Creator, Sustainer and Dissolver of the worlds."

And from this point of view it is true.

He who knows the secret of this Divine manifestation and Its workings, is not incarnated again. When he leaves his body he realizes the Supreme Oneness. Delivered from passion, fear and anger, absorbed in Pure Consciousness, taking refuge always in Pure Consciousness, many, purified in the discipline of wisdom, have attained complete Self-realization. (9-10)

Any person who fully comprehends the action of the Divine is so purified that he becomes totally Self-realized upon leaving the body and never again has to incarnate against his will. His karma is neutralized as a result of his superior realization.

As men approach me so do I accept them; men of every faith follow the path leading to Supreme Consciousness. (11)

The Eternal Religion meets all men where they are. Every sincere seeker, regardless of his professed religious affiliation and regardless of his method of worship, is striving for spiritual illumination. The desire to know God and understand the proper relationship to all life is universal. Our approach differs because of our concepts, training and early associations. Systems, methods, ways and disciplines vary, and may have usefulness depending upon the needs of those who adopt them.

The four social levels were created from the beginning according to the divisions of quality (of human nature) and ability to work (at the task needing to be done). Though Supreme Consciousness is the creator of these levels, It, Itself, is incapable of action or change. (13)

Supreme Consciousness, in the transcendental aspect, is not involved in action, change, or anything having to do with relativity and duality. But, in the manifest aspect, divisions of responsibility were laid out. Here we are emphasizing, not one's station because of birth, gender, class or education, but rather the individual's aptitude and ability to function. It is quite obvious that not all people are born equal as far as native intelligence or natural ability are concerned. Some, because of their aptitude, can be scientists and educators; others can be involved in business and the variety of career opportunities which are presented in society; some may be suited only for menial labor. Some, for this incarnation, must be taken care of by society. Hopefully, the time will soon come when all people have equal opportunity to express themselves according to their ability, without any prejudice or restriction of any kind.

It is not incorrect for people to gravitate to their own level: that place where they can find their right place in nature's scheme, as well as make their unique contribution. What is unfortunate is for a person, or for a group of people, to try to forcibly play a role for which equal capacities have not yet unfolded. Then, inharmony results and all society is injured. Regardless of the color of a person's skin, regardless of the station of his birth and regardless of the society in which he lives, man is free to do whatever he is divinely impelled to do by virtue of the law of correspondences; that is, whatever

Freedom Through True Knowledge 43

reasonable thing the mind of man can conceive and man can believe, man can experience. Man can be as free as he decides to be, regardless of seeming outside conditions or apparent restrictions. The sages declare that a person's level in society is determined only by his understanding and his conduct, not by anything else. For a person to have to remain in the condition into which he was born is as impractical as it is unspiritual.

A person must work his way through all existing conditions if that is his challenge in life, or he must be free to rise above them if his destined station is a higher one.

> Some devotees offer as sacrifice their material possessions, their self-discipline or their spiritual exercises, while others of subdued minds and strong determination and resolve offer their learning and knowledge. Others, again, who are devoted to life-force control, having restrained the movements of the alternating flow of vital forces in the body, neutralize this flow and rise beyond the body and mind into the awareness of Transcendental Being. Know that all such actions are born of the need to work (to be involved with the law of causation) and this knowledge will free you. (28, 29 and 31)

Here, sacrifice means the surrendering of something in order to gain a higher end. Really, it results in transmutation of the human into the Divine Substance. Some give their all to the spreading of truth teachings. Others discipline themselves and practice spiritual exercises or techniques to clear the mind and consciousness. Others offer their knowledge to the world where it will do the most good. Then, there are those who sit in meditation and actually neutralize the flow of positive and negative (by polarity) vital forces and transcend bodily identifications for a duration as they realize Pure Consciousness. In other words, a person must start from where he is and do something, even if it is merely a matter of making the effort to recall his divine nature, if he is to be free. Whether we exert considerable effort or whether we work with an understanding of the laws of mind and consciousness, we must perform some action to gain our ends. Even the inner agreement and willingness to surrender that which is not useful to higher purposes is an action, because it is a decision that we make, followed by release and acceptance.

> Learn by humble reverence, by inquiry and by service, the knowledge which can be yours. The men of wisdom who have seen the truth will instruct you in knowledge. (34)

Until we realize the God within we can do no better than to follow the advice and example of those who are enlightened. But it is not enough to follow blindly what is written in the scriptures or what is spoken by a spiritual teacher. We must use reason and intuition to know the truth for ourselves; then only will we be completely satisfied. An ancient axiom is, "He who has no personal knowledge but has only heard of many things cannot understand the meaning of scriptures, even as a spoon has no idea of the taste of soup." The Buddha said, "Only he who lives the life shall know the doctrine." That is, we must examine the words of wisdom and then realize them and incorporate them into daily expression if they are to be truly our own.

Here is the key: we must combine devotion to the teacher with the unrestricted right of free examination and inquiry. Blind obedience to authority which results in continued spiritual ignorance is not the way of wisdom. Death of the intellect is not a condition for spiritual insight. Today, there are many pseudo-gurus who draw the gullible to themselves because of their charisma and through the use of modern publicity methods. The people who are drawn are, for the most part, the simple-minded, those who pursue novelty, excitement and the "different." The ancient tradition insists on honest inquiry and sincere reflection. Intellectual apprehension is only the beginning; the initiate must tread the inner path. Faith comes first, then knowledge, then direct experience. Those who have experienced the truth are qualified to guide mankind. Such knowers of truth are true gurus. A guru is one who rests in the

Freedom Through True Knowledge

inner awareness of his Divine nature and whose only purpose in life is to awaken souls and show them the way to freedom. He has no other motives and no other reason for being. There are many teachers who share their acquired information, but there are few true gurus in the world. The words of Plato are appropriate here: "A man should persevere till he has achieved one of two things: either he should discover the truth about them for himself or learn it from someone else; or, if this is impossible, he should take the best and most irrefragable of human theories and make it the raft on which he sails through life."

> When you know this truth, you shall not fall again into confusion, for by this you shall see all manifestations without exception in the soul, then in Supreme Consciousness. Even if you should be the most blind of souls you shall move through this blindness as the result of wisdom. As the fire consumes the fuel, so wisdom burns all karma. He who has faith, who is established in wisdom and who is self-disciplined, gains greater wisdom, and having gained this attains supreme peace. Therefore, having cut asunder with the sword of wisdom the doubts of the heart, born of ignorance, practice Yoga (the science of Self-realization) and awaken to the realization of the Supreme Self. (36-37, 39 and 42)

We should, according to the *Gita*, perform all actions in this world with the help of knowledge and concentration. Any doubt is the product of ignorance, and this will be erased when enlightenment is experienced. Then we will automatically know what is right in all circumstances.

One will notice that renunciation is emphasized in these scriptures, but we only renounce a lower action for a higher one or one way of doing things for a better way.

Chapter Five

FREEDOM THROUGH PERFECT RENUNCIATION

As we have learned, a true renunciate does not give up involvement with the things of the world but merely ceases to rely upon any external thing in favor of reliance upon the Infinite Intelligence. Therefore, to give up our reliance upon externals in favor of That which is the True Cause and Sustainer is the wisest thing to do.

Arjuna speaks:

> You praise both renunciation of works and, at the same time, so it seems, their unselfish performance. Tell me clearly which is the better way? (1)

As we have learned, even enlightened people work, even though there is no karma which impels them. What they do is their own business. Some enlightened masters seem not to work. They remain in seclusion and appear to do nothing at all. Ramana Maharishi, the guru of Paul Brunton, was one of these. Yet, his presence surely illumined the world, and he did work with those who were drawn to him in south India. Even masters who have no mission in society "work" through their meditations and because they remain embodied and clear human consciousness, though this is not fully understood by people who cannot fathom why such people, with all of their wisdom, should choose such lives. It is a matter of destiny. An enlightened soul follows inner guidance, always.

Arjuna's question, scholars feel, is for the unenlightened person for, obviously, if he were enlightened he would not ask the question; he would know the answer. The intention of the *Gita* seems to be to spell out the fact that we are to abandon selfish work which binds us, and not to abandon all activity.

Freedom Through Perfect Renunciation

Works alone cannot save us (from ignorance) but intelligent activity is not contrary to wisdom.

Krishna answers:

Both the renunciation of works and their unselfish performance lead to salvation. But of the two, the unselfish performance of works is better than their renunciation. He who neither loathes nor desires should be known as one who has the true spirit of renunciation; for, free of the dualities, he is easily released (from bondage). The ignorant speak of renunciation and the practice of works as being different, but not the wise. He who applies himself to one, gets the fruits of both. The status which is obtained by men of renunciation is reached by men of action also. The person who sees clearly sees that the ways of renunciation and of action are one and the same. But renunciation is difficult to attain without the practice of Yoga; the sage who is earnest in Self-realization through action soon attains to the realization of the Absolute. (2-6)

Many years ago, while living as a monk and undergoing training with my guru, Paramahansa Yogananda, I worked many hours a day to help maintain the organization. I found, as Yoganandaji said I would, not only a sense of fulfillment as a result of useful work, but also that my body was suitably tired and relaxed at day's end so that meditation came more easily. In fact, the first thing that Yoganandaji said to me, during my initial interview with him was, "This path is not a path of escapism, you know!" True yoga practice involves the use of will and discipline so that we perform our work, whatever it is, in the right spirit and with the correct attitude. The paths of pure knowledge and involved action are not inconsistent. In the former we renounce alien thoughts and feelings; in the latter we will (and work) them away.

The secret of freedom in this world is to live without grasping and without rejecting; taking things as they come or seem right, according to our attitude and condition of consciousness. Actions performed by both the unaware and the enlightened may seem to be the same, from an outside point of view, but the inner attitude and realization are very different.

But true renunciation is difficult to attain without self-discipline (yoga practice); the sage who is serious in non-attached action attains the realization of God quickly. He who is trained in this way (of renunciation) and is pure in soul, who is the master of his nature and who has conquered the senses, whose soul realization is that he is aware of himself as the life of all beings, he is not tainted by works, even though he is active. The man who is aware that he is a divine being and who knows the truth thinks, "I do nothing at all," for in doing all things he knows that it is a sense-perception only that is involved with things of the world. He who works in this manner is not touched (influenced) by anything of the world. (6-10)

Even though a person works for the good of the world, if he does so with the right attitude, as the servant of all, he is free, even while working. Things change from moment to moment, but that which is Real never changes. A prince once asked a jeweler to inscribe in the band of his ring something that would stand by him in times of good fortune and bad; the inscription when completed read as follows: "This, too, will pass away."

Thus it is with all phenomenal things. The sure way to freedom is to erase ego: the sense of separateness. And this is done as we work without selfish motivation, as hard as this might be, in the beginning, to comprehend, or do. When we get down to the basics, there is nothing but the One, in an almost infinite variety of expressions.

The karma-yogins (men of action) perform works merely with the body, mind, understanding, or the senses, abandoning all attachment, for the purification of their souls.

Freedom Through Perfect Renunciation

> The true devotee attains to peace by giving up attachment to the results of work, but he who is not Self-realized is impelled by desire, and is attached to the results of action and is bound. (11-12)

"Teach me your mood, O patient stars," writes Emerson, "Who climb each night the ancient sky, leaving no space, no shade, no scars, no trace of age, no fear to die!" Ralph Waldo Emerson was a deep student of the Vedas, the scriptures of ancient India, and his writings reveal this ever so clearly. Would that we all might emulate the stars and "leave no space, no shade, no scars, no trace of age, no fear to die." Would that we all might be able to give up our self-seeking and dissolve the ego so that the Spirit could fully express Itself! Even though we have been in darkness for ages, when the Divine Light breaks through, surely everything will be made clear, bright and altogether worthwhile.

> The embodied soul who has controlled his nature, having renounced all actions by the mind (through inner discipline), dwells at ease in the city of nine gates (the body with its nine openings, i.e., ears, eyes, nostrils, mouth, and organs of excretion and generation), neither working nor causing work to be done. The Supreme Self does not create for human beings, nor does It act (for them). Nor does It connect action with effects of actions. It is nature which works on these levels. The All-pervading Spirit does not take on the sin (mistakes due to ignorance) or the merit (blessings due to right action) of any person. Since, in most instances, light is overshadowed by darkness, people are confused. But for those in whom the darkness is banished by light, for them the reality of the Supreme Self is revealed. (13-16)

We (as souls) sit within the body; it is our instrument, it is our vehicle through which we express in this sphere. And, if we are aware of this and in full control, we are not at the mercy of the conflicting urges and desires of the body or mind.

God, in the transcendental aspect, is beyond all duality. Therefore, It does not concern Itself (here, referring to the Absolute) with our human desires or needs. This is a hard matter to accept, for those who have been exposed to the popular teaching trend which declares, in effect, that "God wants man to prosper, to be in health, and to enjoy all manner of success in the world." It is true that God in the aspect of world manifestation is inclined in the direction of the completion of purposes; therefore, a person who is in harmony with the completion of purposes, or God's will, will experience what the world refers to as prosperity, health and success. But the Transcendental Being is not concerned with man's coming and going in this world. It remains aloof from all activities; yet, It is the underlying support of the entire phenomenon.

When we are anchored in the realization of our True Nature we are the witness of all that happens to the body. We move through life as though in a conscious dream, involved but not involved. Participating, but at-a-distance. This is not a matter of split personality; it is a matter of inward recognition of what is taking place moment by moment, while remaining anchored in understanding.

> **Contemplating the Supreme, directing their entire conscious attention to Reality, making Reality their entire aim and with It as their sole object of devotion (surrendered attention), they (disciplined souls) reach a state from which there is no return, their ignorance banished by light, their confusions eradicated by wisdom. Sages (men of true vision) see clearly that the learned and the humble seer, those on the lower rungs of the evolutionary ladder, even the souls which animate animal forms, are in essence the same. (That is, the Divine Essence animates all forms.) The person who is established in the spirit of renunciation, upon giving up his body, is supremely free. (17, 18)**

With practice, the ego is dissolved and soul consciousness is clearly revealed. It is said that a little learning results in dogmatism, a little more results in questioning, and more still, to

Freedom Through Perfect Renunciation

prayer. We learn that we are sustained by something greater than we are. Great thinkers have always become deeply religious. Humility is the most natural result of honest self-inquiry. If we are honest, we must eventually conclude that all lifeforms are animated by the same Light. Wherever there is life, there must also be the expression of the One. If we, for a moment, allow ourselves to think, "God is in man but not in the animals," then we must admit to being double-minded. For is it not our basic theme that "God is all" and "All things were made by Him"? We either stand by our basic principles or we do not! Is not Reality revealing Itself through higher and higher forms, and through successive stages of manifestation? We all have a metaphysical reality which is in common. Wise people see God in all expressions and develop the characteristic of equal-mindedness which is most to be desired.

> Even on earth the world is transformed by those whose minds are established in the vision of oneness. Spirit is flawless and appears the same in all manifestations. When the soul is no longer attached to external things one finds real happiness in Self-realization. He who is thus Self-realized, when leaving the body, is supremely blissful. Shutting out all external things, fixing the vision between the eyebrows (the mystic third eye center), the sage who has controlled the senses, mind and understanding, who is intent on liberation, who has cast away desire, fear and anger, he is forever freed. And, having realized that Spirit is all that is, he (the sage) attains peace. (19, 21, 27, 28, 29)

We can attain liberation on earth if we are properly motivated and in tune with the Supreme Self. When we awaken fully we do not lose anything; we remember the Truth, that we are all that is. By flowing the attention to the third eye center (in meditation) we find release from involvement with externals and move back to the true Source. At this time our attention is one-pointed and all of our energies stream as one, to the End (and Beginning) of life. In this way we rise above the unconscious, subconscious and conscious levels of mind and become aware of pure Existence.

When the moment arrives, as it must for all embodied souls, if we have been attentive to meditation practice and are surrendered to God, with no attachments of any kind, we will move from the body through the spiritual eye or crown chakra and experience the highest and most clear state of which we are capable at that moment. Every time we meditate correctly, we die to the world and awaken more obviously to our true nature. Upon returning to body awareness and this-world relationships, we will live freely because we are true renunciates; we are able to see the Eternal Reality behind the shifting forms and circumstances of the relative world.

Happy indeed is that person who is so established in the conscious awareness of the presence of God that he is stable and appropriate at all times. Such a one is a true saint, and his presence among us is a most special blessing.

Chapter Six

LIBERATION THROUGH MEDITATION

What is meant by true renunciation is disciplined behavior; that is, behavior that is in accord with the highest ideal, while we remain inwardly aware of our changeless nature. In fact, the *Gita* stresses the point that it is better to work in the world with the proper attitude than to remain in seclusion and attempt to repress desires and urges. It is a matter of total surrender of self-centered will, so that the Divine will can have free play through our lives. If we can control our thoughts, we can put an end to unreasoned desires and win peace.

Krishna speaks:

Let a man be elevated by contemplation on the Supreme Reality which exists within himself. For the person who has conquered human nature as a result of contemplation, the inmost Reality is a friend. But for the person who has not realized his true spiritual nature, the inmost Life will seem to be an enemy. When one has overcome the tendencies of his human condition and has attained to the calm of self-mastery, he is anchored in the awareness of his True Nature and in the midst of all dualities he is at peace. (5-7)

Each of us has the freedom of choice: to give in to the impulses of our human nature which, for the most part, have only to do with the senses, or to rise to freedom. Our future is in our own hands. The natural urges of the body are not to be totally denied or suppressed, but intelligently directed. In time, we can be in unity with the Universal Self of all. Our soul nature is ever the same but when it is identified with the tendencies in nature its freedom is hampered. To the degree that we are able to regulate our activities and remove obstructions from the mind and consciousness, soul consciousness can express freely.

The single-minded initiate whose soul is satisfied with wisdom and knowledge, who is unchanging and master of his senses, to whom all outer manifestations seem an expression of the same basic substance, is said to be in full control. He who is equal-minded among friends, companions and foes, among those who are neutral and impartial, among those who are hateful and related, among saints and sinners, he excels. (8-9)

A single-minded person is one who sees Reality behind the ever-changing appearances of the world. Regardless of outer appearances, regardless of surroundings, regardless of the people with various motives and views with whom he associates, such a person is always the same. It is not that he is cold and indifferent, but rather that he is possessed of a deeper understanding.

Let the practitioner of yoga try constantly to concentrate his mind on the Supreme Reality, remaining in solitude and alone, self-controlled, free from desires and longings for possessions or sense experience. Having his body positioned in a firm posture, let him make his mind one-pointed; controlling thoughts and senses, let him practice pure contemplation in order to attain inward purity. Holding the body, head and neck erect and still, flowing the attention to the third eye (the place between the eyebrows) without allowing his eyes to wander, serene and fearless, firm in his vow of self-control, subdued in mind, let him sit, harmonized, his attention flowing to the Transcendental Field which is the Single Reality. The devoted person of controlled mind, ever remaining harmonized, attains to peace, the supreme realization. (10-15)

This is the ideal description of the way of meditation. The

instruction here given is in agreement with the instruction as given by Patanjali in the classic text on Raja Yoga, *The Yoga Sutras of Patanjali*. Ordinarily, a person's attention flows out into the world and he becomes entangled in the affairs of the world as a result. Proper meditation practice enables a person to reverse the flow of attention and vital force, for the duration of the practice, so that the inner realms can be more easily explored. It is suggested that a steady creative effort be made in the direction of superconscious experience as the result of meditation.

Unless we are alone, away from possible distractions, it is almost impossible to fully concentrate and achieve the desired results. True meditation is a beyond-the-mind experience; as Boehme wrote, it is a matter of "stopping the wheel of the imagination and ceasing from self-thinking." Rilke, in his *Letters to a Young Poet*, wrote, "I can give you no other advice than this, retire into yourself and probe the depths from which your life springs up."

Again, I emphasize that we are not to permanently withdraw from the world. But we must have time in which to get to know ourselves as we really are, unfettered by all of the emotional and psychic conflicts which we are prone to experience.

Sometimes, in these verses, the translation suggests that a person in meditation focus his attention on the tip of the nose. What is really meant, in the original Sanskrit, is the origin of the nose, the place between the eyebrows, the psychic center popularly known as the third eye. This is a true act of repentance, a going back to the Source of life within the body. When Pythagoras was questioned about why he called himself a philosopher, he responded with the following story. He compared human life to the great festival at Olympia, where all the world comes together in a mixed crowd. Some are there to do business at the fair and enjoy themselves. Others wish to win the wreath in the contest; others are merely spectators, and these last are the philosophers. It is declared by true spiritual teachers that the essential qualifications of an initiate-to-be are a capacity to discriminate between what is eternal and what is non-eternal, detachment, self-control, and a strong yearning for spiritual freedom.

The masters of India, in teaching the concept of celibacy, did not mean total abstinence from sexual intercourse. What they stressed was right use of all energies and right direction of thought. A person in the world who lives a normal life but who meditates and works with the realization that the One Life is working through, and as, him is a true sage.

The spiritual life is not a life of praying and petitioning God. It is the life of self-surrender which results in a clearing of the consciousness so that the Divine can function through the human organism with little or no restriction.

The path which leads to Self-realization is not for the person who overeats or, on the other hand, fasts too much. It is not for the person who sleeps too much or sleeps hardly at all (as an act of penance). For the person who is temperate in taking food and in his recreational pursuits, who is controlled in his actions, whose habits are regulated, a natural discipline results which destroys all sorrow. (16, 17)

What the *Gita* calls for is balance and intelligent human behavior. The middle path of the Buddha and the golden mean of Aristotle are the same ideals. People who go to extremes reveal a subconscious desire to somehow merit the grace of God because of zealous behavior, or they act out of compulsion to harm themselves because of guilt feelings or a sense of inadequacy.

Now follows a discourse on what constitutes a perfect seeker on the path.

When the disciplined mind is established in the realization of the True Self (the soul) and is liberated from all desires, a person is said to be harmonized in his practice. As a lamp in a windless place does not flicker, to such is compared the mind of a self-controlled practitioner of meditation. In that condition in which he finds supreme joy, perceived

Liberation Through Meditation 57

by the intellect and beyond the reach of the senses, therein established, he no longer falls away from realization. Gaining that supreme vision beyond which there is no greater gain, he is firmly established and is not shaken by the darkest sorrow. Let this condition of consciousness be known as true Self-realization. This experience should be continued with determination, without faltering and without regret. Whatever tempts the mind to waver, let it be overcome and let the attention be focused on the Supreme Reality. For the highest happiness comes to the person whose feelings are at rest, whose consciousness is cleared, and who has realized his True Nature. In this way, the devotee who has seen through error experiences easily the infinite bliss of God-realization. (18, 19, 21, 22, 26, 27)

To succeed in meditation we must release everything which stands in the way of our perception and experience of clear awareness. All feelings of regret, resentment, guilt, fear, prejudice, attachment, longing, and egotism must be resolved, for they are not a part of true divine consciousness. We must even rise beyond mental pictures, including our favorite concept of God. The law is: we become what we contemplate. Or, we assume the viewpoint of that which we contemplate. We are already pure, bright, all-powerful and all-wise, but we have to accept this to be true and look out upon the world with clear vision. Although attempts to account for mystical experiences reflect racial and cultural temperaments, the illumination of Hindu and Buddhist seers, of Socrates and Plato, of Christian and Muslim sages, are all similar. The cosmic vision is universal because Reality is one.

The person who sees Spirit everywhere and sees all things in Spirit; he is self-contained and Self-realized. He who sees everything as a manifestation of himself, regardless of circumstances, he is considered a perfected seer. (30-32)

This is true cosmic consciousness, to see everything in the world as an expression of the One, without exception. Perfect love (non-judgmental respect) is born of this vision.

Arjuna, like anyone else to whom the idea of meditation is new, has a question:

> This practice you talk about, stressing evenness of mind, I see no possibility of because of mental restlessness. The mind is very fickle; it is impetuous, strong and obstinate. It seems as difficult to control as the very wind itself. (33-34)

The reasoning has not changed through the ages. Even today, after meditation is fully explained to a person, a question is invariably asked, "But what about the restless mind? I cannot control it!" So, the instruction must continue:

> Without a doubt the mind is difficult to curb and is restless, but it can be controlled by constant practice and non-attachment. Self-realization is hard to attain by a person lacking in discipline; but by the self-controlled it is attainable, if one strives through proper means. (35, 36)

Any person who is willing to make an inner agreement with himself to meditate can soon learn to practice with benefit. Of course, some find it more of a challenge than do others. But, all can succeed through right effort and proper means. This is why a guru is often necessary, so that the student can be properly instructed. Just to sit and watch thought processes, use affirmations to condition the mind, or to sit and wait for something to happen, is both unscientific and of little use.

Arjuna has yet another question:

> What about the person who cannot control the mind, even though he has faith (in the practice), and who fails in his attempt to attain Self-realization? What is his destiny? Does he perish like a cloud rent in the sky by the winds, is he left in limbo, missing both this life and life eternal? (37, 38)

Liberation Through Meditation 59

A valid question indeed! Is there any purpose in starting on the spiritual path if one cannot succeed in this incarnation?

Krishna counsels him:

> Arjuna, neither in this incarnation nor in the hereafter is there destruction for the person who is rightly resolved; for never does a person who endeavors to be good tread the path of woe. Having attained (in the astral realms, after leaving the body) the world of the righteous and having dwelt therein for many years (in earth time), the person who has fallen away from his spiritual discipline is again incarnated in a desirable environment. He may be incarnated into a family of spiritually aware people, who are endowed with wisdom. There he regains the mental impressions of previous realizations and, with this as his starting point, he strives again for perfection and full realization. As a result of his former practice he is carried irresistably forward. Such a seeker of truth goes beyond the rule of scriptures (the letter of the law). The sincere truth seeker who strives without slackening, cleansed of all karma, perfecting himself through repeated incarnations, then attains the highest goal. Such a Self-realized person is considered to be greater than ascetics; he is greater than the man of knowledge (only), greater than the man who is bound by rituals; therefore, become Self-realized. And of all such Self-realized persons, he who is full of faith and who is established in Pure Consciousness, I consider him to the the most attuned to this teaching and anchored in the Divine. (40-46)

Here is hope for all who have ever wondered about their future on the spiritual path! Here the truth is revealed: souls continue in their progress, incarnation after incarnation, until full realization is experienced. For this reason, even if progress seems slow, or even non-existent, we should strive with the best that is in us. Eckhart wrote, "If thou do not fail in intention, but only in capacity, verily, thou has done all in the sight of God."

A few years after we take on a fleshly body, the dormant subconscious memories (mental impressions) come to the surface of the mind and act as reminders to us and urge us onward. Some people, fortunately, awaken to a sense of soul awareness at an early age and begin their conscious quest. Others likewise awaken but suppress the urge because it does not seem appropriate in their new surroundings. While all forms of practice are considered worthwhile—the way of renunciation, the way of knowledge, the way of selfless work, Krishna declares that the superior person is the one who is firmly established in the realization of God through faith and devotion.

Chapter Seven

GOD AND CREATION

In this chapter Krishna endeavors to enlighten Arjuna concerning that which is beyond the body: the manifest worlds.

> Listen now, how as a result of proper study and practice, with the attention anchored in God, you can know the fullness of Reality without doubt. I will explain this wisdom together with knowledge, and by knowing this there is nothing else to be known. Among thousands of men scarcely one strives for perfection and of those who strive and succeed (in some measure) scarcely one among them really knows the Final Truth. (1-3)

Here is the promise: it is possible for a person to be a knower of the truth about life. Only one person out of a thousand even tries to experience Self-realization, and of the ones who strive, very few really know the Ultimate Reality. If we identify ourselves with the masses we are likely to become fainthearted and give up soon after we begin. But if we maintain the proper self-image and affirm, "If ever one other person before me has attained to Self-realization, I will," we are more likely to persist and by persisting, succeed on the path.

Krishna is here revealing, not only the nature of Transcendental Being, but also how this Being appears in and as the world. Even though God appears in and as nature and in and as man, God is not limited in any way. Most people are impelled through life by the voice of tradition and authority. Even among the few who become somewhat Self-realized, fewer still learn how to bring their realization into daily expression and to let it express through every fiber of their being.

Earth, water, fire, air, ether, mind and understanding, and self-sense (the sense of individuality)—this is the eightfold division of Spirit as It manifests. This is the lower nature, the manifest nature, of Spirit. You should also know (realize) the higher nature of Reality (Pure Being) which upholds the manifestation. You should know that all beings have their origin in Spirit and that Spirit is the cause of manifestation as well as the cause of its dissolution. There is nothing more pure than Transcendental Being. All manifestation is strung on Spirit as rows of gems on a string. (4-7)

Maya, the fabric of nature, the sense of illusion, is the basis of this objective world. In truth, there is nothing but Consciousness and Consciousness in form. This is our basic premise as we view creation, on whatever level, from the gross to the most subtle. "All things were made by him and without him was not anything made that was made." (*St. John 1:3*) Ego is the sense of separateness which gives rise to the idea of God *and* nature, instead of the truth that Nature is God in manifestation. Universal Being includes the totality of the unconscious and the totality of the conscious. It is all self-contained, even though it appears to be separated. Each person, who is deluded, contains two sides: the real being and the image or concept of self because of identification with creation. In the highest sense, Spirit is the architect, rather than the creator. Everything is formed of one basic substance. For those of the Christian tradition, the general thinking is that Spirit creates everything out of nothing. For knowers of truth, Spirit forms things out of Itself. Here is a difference in viewpoints. The world is not an illusion, but the average person's view and understanding of it constitutes the sense of illusion. The Supreme not only projects the worlds but also dissolves Its own projections. As "gems on a string," so are the worlds strung (owe their existence to) on Spirit.

I am the taste in the waters, I am the light in the moon and sun. I am the mystic sound (Aum, OM, Amen) and I

God and Creation

am the vital force animating all creatures. I am the pure fragrance in earth and brightness in fire. I am life in all manifestations and even the self-discipline which is expressed in knowers of truth. Understand, I am the eternal seed (origin) of all manifestations. I am the intelligence of the intelligent; I am the splendor of the splendid. I am the strength of the strong, free of desire and uncontrolled desire. In all men I am the yearning for truth which is not inconsistent with the law of responsible behavior. (8-11)

Spirit is that which manifests in all expressions. Without It nothing could exist. It is merely a matter of shading, coloring and forming. Desire is not wrong. What is preferred is a yearning for Self-realization and a surrendering of selfishness.

And whatever states of consciousness there may be, be they harmonious, passionate or slothful (elevating, activating, or influenced by inertia) know that they are manifestations of Consciousness. Spirit is not completely represented in them; they are modifications. Most people, deluded by these threefold tendencies, do not perceive the true nature of the Absolute, which is above the tendencies and which is imperishable. This sense of illusion is hard to overcome. But all who contemplate the Supreme Reality pass beyond it. (12-14)

Most people see the manifestations or appearances in this world but not That which is the cause of them: Spirit flowing through the conditioned consciousness of man. The hypnotism of mass consciousness is hard to overcome, according to the *Gita*, but it can be overcome (seen through), and those who contemplate the True Life are successful.

Those who are low on the human scale, the deluded people, whose minds are carried away by the sense of illusion and who identify with negative tendencies, do not seek enlightenment. But the virtuous ones, those who seek the truth, are of four kinds: the man in distress, the seeker for knowledge, the seeker of wealth, and the man of wisdom. Of these, the wisest of all, the singleminded person of devotion, is best. He is the nearest to Self-realization. Noble indeed are all seekers but the sage, I feel, is nearest to truth, for being harmonized, he resorts to the realization of Pure Consciousness as the highest goal. (15-18)

People who are negative and restless cannot rise high on the spiritual path. But, for them to observe the rules of proper conduct, as laid down in the scriptures, is the first step in the right direction. Four kinds of people seek truth: those who are in trouble and seek a way out, the person who desires knowledge in order to function better in the world, the person who strives to amass a fortune for the sake of attainment only, and the man of wisdom who desires enlightenment. The last makes the most rapid progress, although any reason for seeking truth is better than none.

At the end of many incarnations, the man of wisdom yearns for the realization of Reality, knowing that in truth, Reality is all that is. Such a person is difficult to find. (19)

After many incarnations of striving and of trying the various ways which seem best, a wise person renounces useless procedures and surrenders all in order to awaken and know himself as Pure Consciousness. These individuals are rare on earth, but they are becoming more and more numerous in our awakening New Era.

Those whose minds are distorted by selfish desires resort to other gods (images or ideas), observing various rituals, in bondage to their lower nature. However, whatever form any sincere person with faith wishes to use as a focus for his devotions, Spirit makes that faith firm. Endowed with faith a person seeks the favor of a lower ideal and still obtains his wish; the result is due to the response of Life alone. However, such results are temporary to those men

God and Creation

of narrow-mindedness. The worshippers of the gods go to the gods but the worshippers of Spirit awaken to the realization of Pure Being. (20-23)

Deluded people worship concepts of God which seem real to them and, to a degree, according to their faith, their prayers are answered. It is still the movement of Consciousness in and through their lives according to their simple faith. Those who contemplate (and believe in) the gods of their imaginations, identify with them after this incarnation. They become one (for a time) with their own imaginings. But the people who "worship in spirit and in truth" awaken to life eternal.

Deluded people think of Consciousness as being in manifestation only, not perceiving the higher nature which is changeless and transcendental. Because Reality is veiled by the sense of illusion (maya), It is not clearly realized by all people. Thus, those who are deluded do not comprehend the truth that Consciousness is, in Its transcendental aspect, unborn and unchanging. Spirit is conscious (in Itself) of all manifestations, past and present. All individualizations (souls which are embodied) are involved with the sense of illusion and the relativities and dualities. But those who tread the path of Self-realization, who have neutralized their karma and overcome (seen through) the sense of illusion, are forever in full awareness of the Truth. They transcend the concepts of old age and death and know That which is beyond action and involvement. Those who realize Spirit as all in all, governing both material and subtle aspects, and all actions, know the ultimate Truth at the time of leaving the body. (24-30)

Everything we perceive through the senses is a projection, a manifestation on the screen of time and space. It is caused by, and we perceive it because of, maya. *Maya* is a term referring to the basic cause-substance of which the worlds are formed. Its components are: creative energy, light particles, space, and time. The world we perceive through the senses is real, in that it is Consciousness appearing-as. But there is more to the process than we perceive through the senses. There is a higher order of Reality which exists and which can be comprehended. All people who are embodied are to a degree deluded, and because of this they do not have the intuitive sense which enables them to comprehend the truth about life directly. The ideal, according to the sages, is to plan our entire life toward the eventual moment of experiencing Reality. We need not relate all of our spiritual practices to preparation for eventual transition, but the teaching is that if we live properly, with the right attitude and in the right consciousness, when the time comes for us to make our transition we will move from this world into full realization of Truth Consciousness.

Chapter Eight

THE PATTERN OF COSMIC UNFOLDMENT

Arjuna now asks some basic questions:

What is the nature of the Absolute (Transcendental Being)? What is the truth about the soul and what is the nature of action (movement)? What is the domain of the elements and of the gods? What is the domain of transmutation (from lower to higher) and how is Spirit to be clearly realized or apprehended at the time of leaving the body by those who seek the truth? (1, 2)

The rush of questions is characteristic of a person who is new on the path and who wants to know everything at once, often on his own terms, to his own satisfaction, and without delay! The beautiful thing is that all questions can be answered fully.

Krishna begins:

The Absolute is indestructible and supreme; individualized Spirit is referred to as the soul. Karma is the name given to the creative force that brings all manifestations into expression. The basis of all manifest forms is the combination of tendencies in nature; the basis of all transmutation (from lower to higher) is inherent in Spirit. And whoever, at the time of departure from the body, contemplates Spirit alone, he experiences absolute freedom. According to what man contemplates at the moment of leaving the body, he becomes aware of upon moving into the astral, causal, or celestial realms. Therefore, at all times contemplate Pure Being and persist. When the attention and insight are firmly set on Pure Consciousness you will realize Pure

Consciousness without doubt. He who contemplates Reality as a result of constant practice, who does not think of anything else, he realizes the Truth. He who contemplates the pure Light which is behind darkness (maya) at the time of leaving his body, centering his attention and life force at the spiritual eye, attains full enlightenment. (3-10)

Spirit is pure existence, without any qualification or conditioning. The soul is individualized Spirit. Creation is the result of Spirit's self-modification. If we, at the time of the last breath, flow the attention and feeling to the spiritual eye and yearn to know the Ultimate Truth, we will rise above all karmic identifications and experience our nature as Light and Life. This is the quickest way to freedom, but it is hard to accept for the average person who is restricted in his believing and who thinks in terms of working out his karma, growing through experience and learning one step at a time. The truth is: we came from Light, our nature is Light, and when we become free from all delusive thoughts we will know ourselves as Light.

Let me describe that state of consciousness which seers call unchangeable, which Self-realized people enter and which causes them to be self-disciplined. With the senses under control, the attention properly directed, the life force flowing to the spiritual eye, firmly established in pure contemplation, such a person, merging with the cosmic sound current, contemplating Spirit, experiences Pure Consciousness. He who constantly contemplates Reality, thinking of nothing else, and who is ever self-disciplined, by such a person Truth Consciousness is easily experienced. Having realized their true nature, such souls do not return to the body, for they have attained the highest perfection. (11-15)

When a person becomes proficient in the practice of deep meditation, he has control over his thoughts, energies, and even the trend of experience after leaving the body. This scripture declares that the vital forces leave the body through the spinal cord, into the crown chakra (upper brain), and from there pass out of the physical form. In this way, various levels of mind are bypassed and the soul awakens to clear awareness of itself as Consciousness. In this way a soul experiences freedom and does not have to incarnate again. Souls which identify themselves with any level of creation, from subtle to gross (from celestial realms to the physical plane), are subject to reincarnation. But souls which know themselves as Pure Consciousness are above dualities and are free from involvement with maya, the cause of the sense of illusion.

> From the realm of Light downwards, all worlds (have in their nature) the tendencies which cause re-embodiment. But, upon realizing itself as Pure Consciousness, the soul does not incarnate again. (16)

As long as a person is identified with creation, on any level, he is somewhat at the mercy of the forces in nature and will therefore be forced, even against his conscious desire, to play some role in time and space. The only way out of the mortal dream is for a person to awaken from it. The only lesson we have to learn in life is to awaken and become knowers of Truth. Delusion gives rise to all other confused mental states.

> Those who know that the day of God is of the duration of a thousand Ages and that the night of God is a thousand Ages long, they are knowers of day and night. At the coming of the day, all manifested things come forth from the Unmanifested, and at the coming of night they merge in that same source, called the Unmanifested. This very same multitude of existences, arising again and again, merges helplessly at the coming of night and streams forth into being (again) at the coming of the day. (17-19)

The worlds are manifest on all levels in a regular, orderly manner. According to the seers of this enlightenment tradition, a universal cycle is 4,300,560,000 years and measures out a day of creation: the length of time that creation is out-pictured on the screen of time and space. The life span of the whole universe was calculated, by the ancient seers, to be 314,159,000,000,000 years. God, according to the sages whose revelations made possible the *Gita*, is the outward activating and controlling aspect of Spirit; and Spirit, as Pure Consciousness, is forever changeless. This sending forth and calling back of manifestations of Itself is referred to as the outbreathing and inbreathing of God. There is no reason for this; it is simply how the process works.

> But beyond this Unmanifested, there is yet another Unmanifested Eternal Being who does not cease even when all creation is withdrawn. This is called the Imperishable. Souls which realize this condition never again become involved with outward creation. This Reality is the Supreme Nature of all Life. In This all existences abide and This pervades all creation. This can be realized through steady devotion. (20-22)

When the worlds are dissolved, because of the universal cycle coming to an end, the seed-ideas for things exist within the unmanifest consciousness of God. When creation is again spread out and the play begins once more, these patterns enable formless substance to take form again. Souls which have not attained enlightenment during this time of unmanifest rest (for the same duration as was the outward manifestation) remain in an unconscious state and become involved with creation when it begins again, and from there continue on the path to freedom.

But beyond this unmanifest condition, which we know as God, there is Something else which is the cause of it. It is the truly Unmanifest, Pure Being, Transcendental Consciousness. It never changes. Souls which awaken to this perception never again become involved with day and night (creation and dissolution).

The Pattern of Cosmic Unfoldment

Now I will tell you the time in which seekers of truth, when they leave the body, never return and also, the conditions for reincarnation. Leaving the body in a condition of illumination, the soul awakens completely and knows itself as the Absolute. Leaving the body in a condition of delusion and confusion a person goes to the astral realms, as do all such people. The wise person who understands this goes beyond bondage to cause and effect, and attains to the supreme and original status. (23-28)

Those who are of the light, who desire full awareness, and who give up all attachment, literally overcome the world. But people who are deluded, who are involved in ideas of working out karma, going to the astral realms to be with friends and relatives, and who are expecting spiritual rewards because of earthly observance of scriptural injunctions; they are not very aware, and they go to astral realms for a while before incarnating on the planet once more to continue their efforts at realizing Truth.

Chapter Nine

LIBERATION THROUGH MYSTICAL INSIGHT

To you, who do not shrink from this message, I will declare this profound secret of wisdom combined with knowledge, and this understanding will release you from bondage due to ignorance of spiritual truths. This supreme insight, known by direct experience, in accord with the law, is very easy to practice and is universally and forever applicable. People who do not understand this truth and who do not attain enlightenment, after a duration on the spiritual path, give up and return to the old way of life, living as mortals do. (1-3)

Philosophers often contend that, through reason, they have proved the existence of the Supreme Reality. Sages declare they know through intuitive perception. A person can know the Supreme Reality through both the use of reason and of intuition. Reality cannot only be assumed; It can be known. Often an assumption is the first step to the realization of a truth.

All the universe is pervaded by Spirit. All beings abide in Spirit but Spirit does not abide in them. Yet, all beings do not dwell in Spirit; here is the divine mystery. Spirit, which is the source of all beings, sustains the beings but does not abide in them. (4, 5)

The air exists in space but has nothing in common with space, so Spirit contains all manifest forms but is, at the same time, not limited by them. We are here referring to Pure Consciousness. Of course God, the outward force and intelligence, appears as all that is in nature.

Liberation Through Mystical Insight

> All beings (destined for outward expression) pass into nature at the end of a cycle; and at the beginning of the next cycle, Spirit sends them out into expression. This happens time and time again and the multitude of souls are helpless, being under the control of the forces of nature. But these workings do not bind Spirit, which remains ever indifferent and unattached to these actions. Under the guidance of Spirit nature gives expression to all things, animate and inanimate, and by this means the world remains in action. (7-10)

As we have explained earlier in this text, at the end of a phase or cycle, souls are suspended in the basic fabric of nature until the next cycle causes them to go forth again. Even though this happens many times, Spirit, in Its transcendental aloofness, is not involved.

All enlightened teachers have taught that it is a waste of time for us to question the "why" of creation. We cannot say that creation is for the enjoyment of Spirit, because Spirit enjoys nothing; It just is. It is Pure Consciousness, the Cause of creation and the Witness of it, nothing more. Since there are no other conscious entities (all souls being rays of Spirit in varying degrees of delusion) there are no others to enjoy creation. Nor is creation for the purpose of enabling souls to attain liberation; for if there were no creation there would never have been any soul involvement in the first place and, therefore, no need for liberation. Life is as It is and does as It does.

> **People who are deluded do not perceive Spirit which animates all bodies. Disregarding the underlying Reality, such people cling to bodies, to things and to the world. But Self-realized people contemplate the Life within all forms. Such people express the Divine; they remain steadfast on the path; they see Reality in and through everything. (11-14)**

Here, the attitude of an awakened person is emphasized:

he sees God in all things and in all manifestations. It is not possible to have this perception of life unless a degree of soul awakening is experienced. The narration continues:

> Others worship Spirit with wisdom, with the understanding that it is distinct and omnipresent. Spirit is the ritual action and the act of worship, the ancestral oblation and the (medicinal) herb, the sacred hymn and the melted butter (used in ritual), the fire and the offering. Spirit is the father of this world, the mother, the supporter and the grandfather, the object of knowledge, the purifier, the syllable OM and all of the revealed truths. Spirit is the goal, the upholder, the lord, the witness, the abode, the refuge and the friend. Spirit is the origin and dissolution, the ground, the resting place and the imperishable seed. The knowers of the (three) Vedas who drink the nectar of the gods and are cleansed of sin, worshipping Spirit with full surrender, pray for the way to heaven. They reach that holy world and enjoy in heaven the pleasures of the gods. Having enjoyed the spacious world of heaven, they enter (return to) the world of mortals, when their merit (constructive tendencies) is exhausted; thus conforming to the teachings of scriptures and desirous of enjoyments, they obtain the changeable (that which is subject to birth and death). But those who worship Spirit, meditating on Pure Consciousness alone, to them who ever persevere, Spirit brings attainment of what they have not and security in what they have. Even those who are devoted to other gods (other aspects of Consciousness), who worship them with faith, they also surrender to Spirit, though not according to the true law (the highest way). Spirit is the enjoyer of all modes of worship. But these (latter) men do not know the truth about the Transcendental Field and so they fall (from knowledge). (15-24)

All that takes place in the relative spheres is but a play of Consciousness. Souls are drawn to that which they worship, that which they concentrate upon. On the enlightenment path, we awaken to final Truth or we remain this side of clear knowledge, depending upon our purpose and ultimate goal. Only permanent transcendental experience guarantees true liberation. Anything less can be but a temporary experience. Either we transcend the lesser perceptions or, when our momentum wavers, we return to former states of consciousness.

> Worshippers of the gods go to the gods, worshippers of those who are dead go to join them, worshippers of spirits go to the spirits, and those who contemplate Pure Being realize this conditionless existence. (25)

All people, according to their level of understanding, worship something; that is, they think about it and desire union with it. The *Gita* teaches that people who contemplate the shining ones, the gods, join them in the hereafter; those who contemplate the murky astral realms to which unenlightened people go, experience those realms upon leaving the body; and those who contemplate the various higher astral spheres and think them worthy of experiencing, are drawn into them. On the other hand, people who contemplate the highest, the clearest, the best, experience that. There are many people who make it a lifetime practice to wonder about and to try to communicate with, souls who have left this world and who are supposed to be living in astral realms at one level or another. There is no freedom in this pursuit. The astral realms are also illusory in nature, and the people there are likewise partially deluded. If we desire communication with souls on other planes then we are advised to attune ourselves to the gods, the celestial beings, the perfected ones. But, even better than this is the yearning to awaken completely and know the Ultimate Truth.

> Whatever you do, eat, work, give, take, practice self-discipline; do it with the thought that Spirit is doing it through and as you. In this way you shall be freed from positive or negative results of action (karma) and you shall attain complete Self-realization. Spirit is the same in and

through all men (even in lower forms of life). Even if a man of the most vile manner and behavior worships Spirit with good intentions and undistracted devotion, he must be considered as a righteous person because he is highly resolved. Swiftly does this person become a soul of righteousness and obtain lasting peace. Know this for certain, the true devotee never perishes. For all who take refuge in the Transcendental Field, regardless of their social level, they also attain the highest goal. Fix your mind on Reality, be devoted to Reality, worship (surrender to) Reality; with this kind of discipline you shall realize the true nature of Supreme Consciousness. (27-32, 34)

The ego, the sense of being apart from God, is the main problem which faces all unenlightened people. Therefore, what is called for is self-surrender. Such a surrendered person can never feel the slightest bit superior to anyone else, regardless of education, social level, race, religion or family background. The wise person humbly sees the One Life in all forms. It does not matter how low and coarse a person has been; if such a person will forget the past and contemplate the Light, he will be transformed. His sins will be forgiven. His karma will be neutralized. This does not mean that there is an easy escape from the complications we may have created for ourselves but, at least, there is always the possibility of a way out, and the way out of darkness is into the Light.

The color of a person's skin, his physical history, other superficial characteristics, mean nothing in a spiritual sense. To teach people, regardless of their background, to be proud of their race is just as unwise as it is to encourage a sense of inferiority. What matters is not the race or the color of the skin or, for that matter, even previous history, traditions or customs. The important thing is to strike away all ideas of difference and establish the fact that all men are, beyond a shadow of a doubt, brothers because they have a common origin. The common origin is God. The common life is the life of God. To believe otherwise is evidence of ignorance.

All people on the planet will eventually awaken to the

Liberation Through Mystical Insight

realization of the highest Truth and, then, it will be on earth as it is in the harmonious realms referred to as the highest heaven.

The devotee on the path who remains centered in the awareness of his true nature can never fail in his quest to know God. It is often easy to live a calm life when challenge is not present. The person who is established in Self-realization is able to be calm and centered no matter what unfolds about him. Victory is certain for that one who does his very best and remains surrendered to God, always. When we feel the stirrings of the divine nature within us, we are called to freedom.

Chapter Ten

TRUE ONENESS

Here, what is affirmed by Krishna, if comprehended, will clear the mind of doubt and establish the attention firmly upon what is true in the highest sense.

> Now I will reveal to you the Supreme Word. Neither the hosts of celestial beings nor the great sages know any origin of Supreme Consciousness. Supreme Consciousness is the cause and sustainer of celestial beings (gods) and sages. (1-2)

Spirit is the unborn eternal. Though It has no beginning, all beings with beginning and end derive their existence from Spirit. Spirit is ancient, yet even this cannot be really true because concepts of time do not apply to It. Everything comes out of the Transcendental Field and everything returns to It.

> He who clearly realizes the nature of Consciousness, he alone is undeluded and free from bondage. Understanding, knowledge, freedom from bewilderment, patience, truth, self-control and calmness; pleasure and pain, existence and non-existence, fear and fearlessness; non-violence, equal-mindedness, contentment, austerity, charity, fame and ill-fame are the different states of being which proceed from the Unmanifest Field alone. (3-5)

All states and manifestations of Consciousness issue forth in accordance with the karma of individuals. Though Spirit is unaffected by the oppositions of the world It guides the world to its sure destiny.

True Oneness

The seven great sages of old, and the four lawgivers, are of Spirit. From these first beginnings all else came forth in the world. He who knows in truth this glorious manifestation and of the flow of uninterrupted power of the Supreme, is in tune with, and one with, the Supreme. (6, 7)

All scriptures refer to seven ruling spirits before the throne of God. These are the seven modifications of Spirit, in order for Consciousness to change in frequency and manifest as the entire world process. The lawgivers are embodiments of divine wisdom who set forth to men the rules of orderly behavior and interaction.

The Transcendental Field is the origin of all things and all forms proceed from It. True students of the path fix their attention on Pure Consciousness and surrender self-will, enlighten each other with constructive conversation, and remain content in the realization of the Truth. Out of compassion for people Spirit banishes darkness from human consciousness with the Light of Itself. (8, 9, 11)

God is the cause as well as the material (basic substance) of the world. Dedicated truth students think only of spiritual matters and, at times, share occasions of fellowship wherein they enlighten one another. In this activity they find their greatest contentment. People who are God-centered become magnetized, and this draws a greater light into their lives which dissolves all darkness and heaviness. Over and over again we are reminded that single-minded devotion results in illumination of consciousness.

Arjuna is still inquiring as to the fullness of the divine manifestation. He asks:

Tell me of spiritual manifestations. How may I know Spirit by meditation? What are the various aspects of Spirit to be known by me? Tell me more of the power and method of manifestation. (16-18)

Arjuna is filled with questions and does not tire of hearing words of wisdom from his guru, Krishna.

Krishna answers:

> Now I will reveal to you some divine forms of Consciousness, but only a few of these manifestations because, in fact, they are endless. Consciousness is the true reality of all creatures. It is the cause of all life. It appears as the sun, the stars and the moon. It is revealed in the purest of the scriptures (regardless of their origin); It is the highest of the gods; It manifests as the mind and awareness of all creatures. It, indeed, manifests as all things. It manifests as priests and even as the leaders of wars; It manifests as the greatest of sages and as the cosmic sound current. Consciousness is the cause of (seeming) beginning and (seeming) end of creation. The Life of Consciousness maintains law and order in the worlds. Consciousness is all in all! This entire universe is supported by only a fraction of the reality of the allness of Spirit. (19-42)

While Reality expresses through all manifestations It is more obvious in some manifestations than in others, depending upon how clear the entity's awareness is. Reality expresses through everything that is in manifestation, without exception.

Krishna implies that there is no end to the manifestations of Consciousness. Beyond this solar system there are galaxies, and beyond them other unique spheres of creation on the physical, electrical, and mental levels. The human mind cannot even begin to fathom the magnitude of the workings of Consciousness. This sphere of expression, this material world we perceive, is supported by only one ray of the Supreme Light.

Chapter Eleven

COSMIC AWARENESS

Arjuna declares:

The supreme mystery which has just been revealed to me has banished my confusions and cleared my mind. But, now that the supreme secret has been told to me, I desire to actually see, for myself, and experience Cosmic Consciousness. If you feel it is possible for me to experience this grand vision (to perceive directly) then open my eyes. (1-4)

This is the great moment, when human consciousness is ready to be transformed and Pure Truth is about to be perceived by the inquiring soul. We all, at some stage of unfoldment, stand at this place and become ready for the vision of visions. Now that Arjuna is receptive, Krishna, with his supernatural power, reveals the Ultimate Truth about life and the world process.

The forms of Spirit are a hundredfold, a thousandfold (without number), and are various in kind, shapes and colors. The whole universe is all unified in Consciousness. But man cannot comprehend this, so (to make the cosmic vision possible) Divine sight will be given to the seeking soul. (5-8)

The manifestations of the One are without number and the ordinary mortal, even with good intentions, cannot grasp the magnitude of the many worlds and the many expressions. For this realization, awakened intuition is required, and even this is due to the grace of God.

Saint Hildegard (1098-1180) reported a vision in which she became aware of a "form" who declared his identity as being similar to Krishna in the *Gita*: "I am that supreme and fiery force that sends forth all the sparks of life. Death has no part in me, yet do I allow it, wherefore I am gathered about with wisdom as with wings. I am that living and fiery essence of the divine substance that glows in the beauty of the fields. I shine in the water, I burn in the sun and moon and stars. Mine is that mysterious force of the invisible wind. I sustain the breath of all living. I breathe in the verdure and in the flowers, and when the waters flow like living things, it is I. I formed those columns that support the whole earth...All these live because I am in them and am of their life. I am wisdom... Mine is the blast of the thundered word by which all things were made. I permeate all things that they may not die. I am life." These utterances make it seem as though Saint Hildegard had read, and been influenced by, the very scriptures with which we now deal. In the Christian Bible we read, "No man has seen God at any time." The message is the same: no one in mortal (limited) consciousness can clearly perceive the real Truth.

At this point in the narration, an *observer* makes his comments and describes the happenings from his vantage point:

> Having thus spoken, Krishna (master of Yoga) revealed the Ultimate Truth to Arjuna. Arjuna (the receptive soul) perceived Spirit in all expressions; all divisions, spheres, dimensions and planes were seen to be expressions of the One. If the light of a thousand suns were to blaze forth all at once in the sky, that might resemble the splendor of the Supreme Reality. (9-12)

Arjuna was overcome with awe and reverence. At such a moment in one's personal experience about all he can do is to stand transfixed. The cosmic vision is too overwhelming. Although it has been expected, its impact is great indeed!

Arjuna speaks:

> In the body of Spirit I see all the gods (celestial beings) and every other manifestation as well: God, the many spirits before the throne (the subdivisions of Conciousness which make possible world manifestation), and the powers and forces in nature. I see these as infinite in number and it seems (to me) there is no end. I see the radiance of Spirit, as of a flaming fire. I see Reality which is imperishable and as That which is to be realized. I see Spirit as the original Being. The space between heaven and earth (the subtle and gross realms) is pervaded by Spirit. I perceive that bands of enlightened ones merge in Spirit with a sense of reverence. All worlds and all people and all manifestations in all worlds are sustained by Spirit, even as I am. As moths rush into the fire to perish there, so do all souls rush to the Transcendental Field and become no more (but awaken to everlasting life). (14-29)

Arjuna begins to sense the truth about the cosmic process. He senses that there is more to human experience than just seeing to the creature comforts. The whole activity and the whole end result is leading to Oneness.

Krishna enlightens Arjuna:

> Within the nature of Spirit is the concept of time. Without this the manifest worlds would not exist. Therefore, awaken and see through maya (the sense of illusion, with the characteristics of time, space, creative force and light particles). Be bold and overcome this major problem. (32-34)

In the *Gita*, Reality is responsible for everything. There is no room for debate concerning a struggle between good and evil, God and the devil. In the *Gita* it is clearly explained that Reality is the cause of, and is responsible for, everything.

How are we to reconcile the seeming opposites: destruction, pain and unhappiness on one side and, on the other side, revelation, ecstasy and supreme happiness? It is all God's drama. God is in and through all manifestation. Behind this world of space-time, interpenetrating it, is a creative purpose which can be understood. It is up to us to try to serve this purpose. Frequently the vision of truth produces in man a sense of unworthiness. When Isaiah saw the Lord sitting upon the throne, high and lifted up, he said, "Woe is me! For I am undone; because I am a man of unclean lips...for mine eyes have seen the King, the Lord of Hosts." People tend to think of Reality in a manner which fits in with their concepts of authority: father, teacher, king, etc. But this "light that lighteth every man that cometh into the world" is our very life, our true being. Therefore, in truth, there is no need for us to stand in awe of it.

Krishna speaks:

> Through the grace of God (due to the soul being in tune with the magnetic attracting current of the Godhead), a person is able to perceive the cosmic truth. But this perception is not the result of study, the giving of gifts, the performance of rituals, or the practice of disciplines. A person should not be afraid as a result of seeing the Ultimate Truth. (47-49)

No external action can result in Self-realization. The clear perception of Reality is the result of the soul's identification with the elevating current which clears the mind and consciousness. We work selflessly so as not to create more karma, but to succeed on the spiritual path we should yearn to know the truth about life, and we should awaken the intuition by which Reality is known.

Krishna continues:

> Reality is difficult to see clearly. Even the gods (shining beings) are eager to see It clearly. The study of scriptures, self-discipline, gift-giving and all actions performed with good intentions will not result in Self-realization (if one expects reward for effort and self-sacrifice). But, by unswerving devotion, Pure Consciousness can be realized. The person who surrenders his all to Spirit, without attach-

ment or self-delusion, realizes the Ultimate Truth. (52-55)

Here we find the essence of the message of the *Gita* as it pertains to devotion and Self-realization. With single-minded devotion, we are to work for the welfare of the world with the attitude that the Eternal Life is expressing in and through us, always. It does not matter what we do, if it is right for us according to our talents and abilities, as long as we serve in the right spirit and our will is to do the will of the Supreme. This is what is asked of us. It is all that can be expected.

The *Gita* does not end here. The Transcendental Vision (for any person) is not the end, but the beginning, of a new life. The challenge for us after perceiving, even in part, this great vision of oneness, is to allow the vision to pervade our consciousness and transmute our lives entirely. A fleeting vision, regardless of its impact, is not complete attainment. Emotional satisfaction or passing experience cannot be the end of the quest.

Chapter Twelve

LIBERATION THROUGH LOVE

Inquiring about whether devotion to a personal concept of God is better than the contemplation of the Unmanifest Field (Pure Consciousness) Arjuna asks:

> Which have the greater knowledge of Yoga (the way to freedom), those who worship the personal aspect of Reality (i.e., God as father, mother, friend, etc.) or those who worship (commune with) the unmanifested Absolute? (1)

Some people feel more comfortable worshipping a personal aspect of God. Arjuna wonders which is the best way. Krishna tries to set his mind to rest and answers his question.

> Those who worship Spirit, possessed of simple faith, they are considered to be more knowledgeable. (They know more about various manifestations of Reality). But those who contemplate the Imperishable, the Undefinable, the Unmanifested, the Omnipresent, the Unthinkable, the Unchanging and the Constant; by restraining the senses, being even-minded, desiring the welfare of all creatures, they also realize the omnipotence of Spirit. Those who try to realize the Absolute have a more difficult path to tread because it is harder for people who are encased in physical bodies to realize the formless Reality. Therefore, if a person will surrender all actions to God and contemplate the nature of Consciousness (in and as creation) he will eventually know the Truth. Such a person dwells in Spirit. If a person cannot contemplate Pure Consciousness he should try to meditate. If this is not possible he should then do good works and offer them to God. Or else,

failing in this attempt, a person can do what work is at hand and renounce any personal desire for gain (from that work). (2-11)

Those who contemplate Reality in Its manifest form (as creation) undoubtedly have greater knowledge (a greater accumulation of data), but those who contemplate Pure Being realize This; that is, they realize as they experience the Absolute. Some people on the spiritual path place great emphasis upon the accumulation of data. But Reality is the real goal. Either path is good and the end is the same. Direct perception of Pure Being is more difficult than perception of Consciousness appearing as the various forms because, as embodied creatures, we are used to thinking, and framing concepts in the mind, in order to draw conclusions and arrive at what we feel to be the end of all questing.

It is a matter of temperament whether we adopt the path of devotion or the path of renunciation (in favor of supreme contemplation). If we are not naturally disposed to meditation, then we must discipline ourselves to practice it. If we cannot, under any circumstances, bring ourselves to practice meditation, then we should do the next best thing and work with the attitude that we are serving God through service to mankind. If this is not possible, we should work without any thought of personal reward whatsoever so that the Divine Will might have an opportunity to enter in and possess us completely.

He who is free from any sense of ill will, who is friendly and compassionate and free from egoism; who is even-minded in all situations; who is ever content, self-controlled and unswerving in his devotion, is sure to become attuned to the Supreme Will. That person who is free of any grasping and any tendency to withdraw from life (who sees life as it is) and who has given up personal desire, is in tune with Reality. That person who has risen above the concepts of good and evil, who treats all people alike and is always even-minded and free from attachment; that person who does not react to blame or praise, who is controlled in his manner and speech, taking life as it comes, is in tune with Reality. Those who, with faith, consider Pure Consciousness as the supreme goal, and who live wisely, are truly in tune with the Infinite. (12-20)

In the words of the *Gita*, devotion which leads to quick perception of Reality is better than knowledge about the relative spheres, and desireless action is better even than devotion because it indicates complete surrender to the workings of a Higher Intelligence. A person of pure devotion gives everything to God. More difficult but quicker is the way of meditation, because it allows Truth to be revealed. But a person who is dedicated to Reality is not a dreamer; everything he does is for the uplift of humanity so that God's will might eventually be manifest on earth. A liberated person is not tied to family or to any community. The world is his home because he functions in the awareness of omnipresence, as God does.

Mahatma Gandhi, when writing his *Songs From Prison*, put forth these beautiful words, echoing the thoughts of Tulsidas:

Grant me, O master, by thy grace
To follow all the good and pure,
To be content with simple things,
To use my fellows not as means but ends;
To serve them stalwartly, in thought, word, deed;
Never to utter word of hatred or of shame;
To cast away all selfishness and pride;
To speak no ill of others;
To have a mind at peace,
Set free from care. and led astray from thee
Neither by happiness or woe;
Set thou my feet upon this path,
And keep me steadfast in it;
Thus only shall I please thee, serve thee right.

Chapter Thirteen

THE BODY, THE SOUL, AND THE FACULTY OF DISCRIMINATION

In this chapter Arjuna wants to know about the composition of creation and That which knows about it. Krishna responds:

> Creation is the body of God and the faculty of discrimination enables a person to clearly perceive the truth about it (creation). Spirit, being the cause and sustainer of creation, knows all about creation. Clear perception as to the nature of creation constitutes pure knowledge. Various sages have taught about creation, through songs and in well-reasoned dissertations. There are twenty-four modifications of Consciousness. Attraction and repulsion (along with pleasure and pain), intelligence and steady yearning to know Truth, are contained within nature and its manifestations. (1-6)

In man we find all expressions: that which led to his involvement with material creation and that which draws all men to supreme freedom. For man to become actualized is the ideal: to see all things in proper perspective and to be able to function as he should. Man, among all manifestations, is that which acts upon nature and which (because of his inner characteristics) brings about worthwhile change. Though the Light which illumines men and the trees and flowers is the same, It appears differently according to Its manner of expression. The One Light, however, flows through man, animals, insects, birds, marine life and growing things.

> Lack of egotism (losing the sense of separate self), giving up the desire to harm any living thing, patience, service

> to the guru, purity (of body and mind), steadiness and
> self-discipline; humility and the recognition that the ideas
> of birth, old age, sickness and death (along with pain) are
> distractions; renunciation and even-mindedness in the face
> of all happenings; steady contemplation of Truth even in
> quiet places and crowds; steadiness in Self-realization,
> insight into the Ultimate Truth—this is affirmed to be
> true knowledge and anything else is considered to be in
> error. (7-11)

These verses are clearly self-explanatory. Krishna continues:

> Now, here is the secret of attaining awareness of eternal
> life. Spirit alone is said to be neither existent nor non-
> existent. (That is, It is beyond human attempt to fathom.)
> In the manifest aspect Spirit seems to have form and all
> of the qualities of the senses; yet It is not limited by this.
> Spirit is That which causes and works through the three
> tendencies in nature (elevating, activating, and the tend-
> ency toward heaviness), yet is free from them. Spirit is
> within and without all creatures, unmoving yet also
> moving. Spirit is far away (subtle) and yet very near (dis-
> cernable when manifesting in grosser aspects or when
> perceived through subtle faculties of perception). Spirit is
> indivisible and yet seems to be divided. Spirit seemingly
> creates, upholds, destroys and recreates. A person who
> comprehends this truth about Spirit is free. The fabric of
> nature, and souls, are without beginning; the bodies in
> nature and their vital forces and tendencies (to move, act,
> react, etc.) are from within the characteristics of nature
> itself. Nature is said to be the cause of action, the source
> of bodies and their movements; and the soul alone is the
> cause of the experience of pleasure and pain. The soul
> which is identified with the tendencies in nature becomes
> attached to them, and this is the cause of spiritual blind-
> ness and the endless rounds of incarnations. The soul is
> said to be that which animates the body and, at the same

time, is the silent witness of all experience. It is, in truth, Spirit individualized, possessing all of the characteristics of Pure Being. A person who is able to realize this and who lives from the center of his being, is free. (12-23)

Life is a series of paradoxes; It appears in, through and as creation, yet It is beyond all manifestation at the same time. This is the manifest, and the transcendental, nature of Spirit. When specialized as a life-unit, Spirit is referred to as a soul. Released from such identification and (its) involvements, It is called the Supreme Self. The "light that lighteth every man" is the Great Light. This Light is our real nature and the purpose of the spiritual path is the realization of It.

When a devoted person identifies with the nature of the Divine, he manifests the characteristics of freedom, love and equality. The *Gita* considers nature and the soul as, respectively, the inferior and superior expressions of Consciousness. From nature we take our forms (bodies), but it is due to the longings of the soul (seeking outwardly or inwardly) that we experience either pain or pleasure, or supreme joy (the result of Self-realization). A person who can live in the world and express fully, remaining soul-conscious and not overly involved, is said to be "free while living in the body." He attains salvation. Such a person is said to be a *jivanmukta:* Sanskrit for "free soul."

> By meditation some people perceive the soul nature; others accomplish the same end by the path of pure knowledge, and still others by selfless works. Others who know nothing of these paths succeed on the spiritual path through pure devotion. Whatever is born, whether animate or inanimate, is the result of union between nature and Spirit. A wise person perceives that all works are done by the tendencies in nature (as powered by Spirit). The Supreme Self is without qualities and is beyond space-time. As the one sun illumines this whole world, so does Spirit light up all of nature. Those who intuitively realize the workings of Spirit through nature

(Itself in modified form) and who understand how souls are eventually released from bondage to nature, they attain full liberation. (24-34)

There are different paths to freedom: through meditation, intellectual inquiry, selfless work, and pure devotion. These ways depend upon the individual's particular psychological make-up and level of awareness. All creation is the result of interaction between Pure Being and Its outward modification, nature. When the confusion about this interaction is seen through by the seeker on the path, then freedom is experienced. One need not leave the body or the world to be liberated.

Some philosophers think that God changes as evolution progresses, but the *Gita* says that God changes not, in spite of outward and seeming evolution. The *Gita* says that only forms change; Pure Being remains ever the same. When we can see that the variety of nature and its development are traced to Pure Being, we assume eternity.

Chapter Fourteen

SPIRIT AND THE THREE TENDENCIES IN NATURE

Krishna speaks:

Here is (again) the supreme wisdom, the highest and best; by knowing this all sages and saints have passed from the sense of being deluded to the highest perfection (complete liberation). Souls who realize this truth are not born (issued forth) at the time of a new cycle; nor are they disturbed at the dissolution of the worlds. God (the first manifestation of Pure Being) is the beginning; the field of God contains all seed-ideas and the birth of all beings results. Like father and mother, Spirit causes God to issue forth all manifestation. (In another sense, nature is the mother and God is the father of all, or That which is the cause of all.) (1-4)

When we completely understand how creation comes into manifestation we can stand to one side with an attitude of detachment, allowing circumstances to be as they are, without being involved in their movements. From Pure Being, Light and Power (God) comes forth; from this, through maya, the fabric of nature, everything else results. Our goal is to realize the Truth. "Be you therefore perfect, even as your Father which is in heaven is perfect." (*Matthew 5:48*)

If we were products of nature we could not ever hope to attain Divine status. But our true nature is spiritual, and it is only for a duration that we are deluded and involved with creation. All forms in creation are the result of impregnation of matter by a spiritual essence. The activity of creation continues until causes and effects are neutralized, until the positive and negative poles perfectly harmonize. Creation is the result of interaction between these polarities. When balance is achieved then creation will cease to be, and Consciousness will be in a condition of rest.

> The three tendencies in nature bind the soul to the body. Of these three, the elevating tendency causes health and eventual illumination of consciousness. However, it, too, binds the soul which seeks happiness and personal fulfillment. The activating tendency binds the soul by causing it to seek sense-gratification and purposeless activity. The tendency toward heaviness (inertia) causes the soul to be negligent, lazy and to seek escape through too much sleep. The elevating tendency will eventually prevail over restlessness and the desire to sleep or be deluded. When dissolution of the universe happens, the soul which is identified with the uplifting tendency will obtain liberation (merge in the Light). Souls which are identified with the tendency to perform purposeless action or who are identified with inertia at the time of dissolution of the worlds, (after billions of years of rest) then incarnate among other souls like themselves (either sense-bound or deluded). The results of good action (identified with the elevating tendency) are pure and in the nature of blessings; those who are active only, because they seek sensation, eventually experience frustration and pain; those who are identified with inertia only find greater dullness and ignorance as the result of whatever they do or think. However, when a person perceives That which is beyond the tendencies in nature he attains objectivity and freedom. When he completely detaches himself from all activities of nature he is free. (5-19)

The three tendencies that run through all of nature are what bind the soul to the world. It is difficult to use English equivalents for the words: *sattva, rajas,* and *tamas.* About the nearest we can come is to refer to them as: the elevating tendency, the activating tendency and the urge toward inertia. Sattva leads to luminosity, rajas to activity and tamas to darkness. Sometimes these three are referred to, in order, as: goodness, passion, and dullness, when reflected in human nature. Sattva contributes to the stability of the universe, rajas to its creative movement and tamas to the decay of things. Tamas also contributes to the cohesiveness of particles which make possible the maintenance of the universe. When the soul identifies with these tendencies in nature it forgets its true existence and begins to use mind, life and body for selfish purposes. To free ourselves from bondage to nature we must rise above these tendencies. We are to sublimate sattva into enlightenment, rajas into self-discipline, and tamas into peace of mind. Even a person who is dominated by the uplifting tendency can be in bondage due to a compulsive urge to do good. A free soul is content with soul-knowledge itself. In most instances we are a combination of all of the tendencies, with one or two being dominant.

If a soul is not free from involvement with nature at the time of the dissolution of the worlds, it then sleeps until creation is sent forth again, and continues its unfoldment. The average person rises to enlightenment through three stages: first he is ignorant, then he seeks after "the things of the world" only, and then he strives for the Transcendental Vision. By being good (ethical) we rise above the two lower tendencies, and from that level we ascend into sainthood or God-realization.

Arjuna asks:

What are the characteristics of a person who has transcended all attachment to the things of nature? How does he succeed in transcending? (21)

The characteristics of one who has succeeded in overcoming the world are similar to those of a person who has become established in God-consciousness.

Krishna explains:

That person who does not react to any indication (in his nature) of enlightenment, activity, or delusion, when they

arise, nor long for these manifestations when they cease to exist; that person who is objective (as though standing apart) and who regards (temporary) pain and (temporary) pleasure alike, who is steady of mind and who sees all manifestations of life as manifestations of the One; that person who is unmoved in times of praise or blame, becomes established in the awareness of his true nature as a Spiritual Being. Spirit alone is immortal and imperishable and the eternal law, and is absolute bliss. (22-27)

A seeker of Truth who is completely Self-contained, who sees the outer appearances as a projection on the screen of time and space, and who rests in the realization of Reality, is free and exhibits the characteristics of such a liberated being.

Chapter Fifteen

THE MYSTICAL TREE OF LIFE

Krishna continues:

Sages speak of the imperishable mystic tree, with roots above and branches below. The fruitage of this insight is clear perception which enables a person to know the truth in scriptures. The branches of this mystic tree extend below and above, nourished by the tendencies in nature, with the objects of the senses as the twigs, and karma results, which binds man to action in the physical worlds. A wise person can cut off this tree (with its attachments to the world) with the strong sword of non-attachment. The way to freedom is to seek awareness of the True Source of all things, from which has come forth this cosmic process known as the universe. Seekers of Truth who are free from pride, delusion and unreasoned attachment to things, who are ever devoted to the will of God and who have risen above the relativities and dualities, experience liberation of consciousness. (1-5)

The mystic tree is the brain and nervous system in the body of man. Soul awareness filters down from above, becoming involved with and attached to, circumstances and objects in the world. The body of man is formed of the substance of nature but the body is animated by the soul, the Real Being: a specialized expression of God. The way to become free from involuntary attachment to the world is to become even-minded and anchored inwardly in the realization of God. God is our larger True Self. The soul is omnipresent, and when it awakens fully it experiences omnipresence.

Neither the sun nor the moon nor any earthly light does light up the realm of Spirit. A fragment of Spirit, having become specialized as the soul (which is eternal), becomes involved with creation and draws to Itself the senses (and body) of which the mind is the sixth (sense). When Spirit (as the soul) incarnates, and when It leaves the body of flesh, It takes the senses and the mind and wanders through space (through various astral and mental spheres). Sages, through meditation, realize the nature of Reality as being independent of the characteristics of nature, but those who lack self-discipline do not experience this awareness. Spirit, entering the worlds, supports all creatures with vital energy; It supports even the plants and all living matter. Spirit is modified as the subtle electricities which digest foods and carry out the various life processes. (6-15)

Transcendental Being is beyond all manifestation and is not touched by it, but the soul, the individualization of Spirit, becomes involved with creation and is, to a degree, influenced by the forces in nature. Body, senses, mind, and intellect are formed of subtle substance in order that the soul might have a vehicle through which to express. It is Spirit which enters into and animates everything in creation, by modifying Itself and expressing as needed as energies, life forces and electricities.

There are two manifestations in this world, the perishable and the imperishable; creation, the outward projection, is perishable, and Spirit in, through and behind it all is imperishable. Yet, there is a transcendent aspect to the nature of Spirit which is forever beyond all form (and discussion). A person who contemplates this truth and becomes aware of it knows the most secret doctrine and become supremely wise. (16-20)

In the world we find form and we find that which animates form: Spirit as all of the forces in nature, and Spirit as the soul. But higher than these is the transcendental aspect of

Spirit, which is changeless and incomprehensible to the most knowledgeable of men. The soul which perceives the truth of this knows all there is to know. For such a one all seeking comes to an end.

It is by patient and steady practice of Yoga that one clears the inner restrictions from the mental field, calms the senses and ascends the mystical tree of life. We have come from heaven to play our roles for a time in the relative spheres. When we are called to return to the Source, which is the pure field of Supreme Consciousness, the journey to final Self-discovery begins. The most secret doctrine is not known to any but the enlightened. It is they who have intuitive perception which enables them to see clearly.

Chapter Sixteen

THE POSITIVE AND NEGATIVE ASPECTS OF THE MIND

Courage, purity of mind, wise use of knowledge, concentration, generosity, self-control and right use of abilities, along with faithful study of scriptures and noble purpose; nonviolence, truth, freedom from anger, renunciation, tranquillity, freedom from finding fault (in others or in circumstances), compassion to all, freedom from envy; gentleness, quiet manner and faithfulness (to others or to a cause), vigor, forgiveness, persistence, selflessness, freedom from the desire to do harm to another, and freedom from excessive pride—these are the natural endowments of a person who is born with a divine nature. (1-3)

The *Gita* recognizes that all men have within them the characteristics of light and darkness. But a person in whom the uplifting characteristics are dominant is said to be a person of divine nature. The path is easier for him because he does not have as much to overcome.

A tendency to show off, arrogance, excessive pride, anger, harshness, and ignorance; these are the endowments of a person with a negative nature. (4)

Some people are naturally (because of previous experiences) born gentle and wise and some are naturally born mean and selfish. We take people where they are and go from there, of course.

The positive (divine) endowments are said to make for quick deliverance (from bondage to the senses) and the negative endowments make for greater attachment and

Aspects of the Mind

trouble. People (such as Arjuna) who incarnate with a preponderance of positive endowments are sure to make good, for they have a spiritual destiny. (5)

When a person manifests the positive characteristics we declare him to be "godly," and when he manifests the negative characteristics he is declared to be "devilish" (unduly influenced by heaviness in nature). There are many people who have some understanding but are dominated by the negative tendencies, and so they are "skillful and selfish in their use of wisdom." They have no moral scruples and no spiritual aspirations.

We have described the nature of divine beings; now let us consider the nature of those who are influenced by negative tendencies. Such people do not know (or seem to care about) the way of renunciation and freedom. Their conciousness is not pure, their conduct is not good (positive) and they are slaves to darkness. Such people are rank materialists who do not comprehend the truth that the world has a spiritual basis. These people are really, because of their ignorance, enemies of the world. They think in terms of destruction instead of orderly unfoldment and the perpetuation of the worlds. They are controlled by insatiable desire, full of hypocrisy, excessive pride and arrogance; they are deluded and have selfish (impure) motives. The gratification of their personal desires is their highest aim in life. Such people seek wealth for wealth's sake. They feel themselves to be the doers of all action and never turn within for higher guidance. Eventually they become bewildered and even more involved with delusion. These people, given to self-conceit, force, and pride, spend incarnation after incarnation in a dark, negative condition. The gateway to pain and seemingly endless delusion is threefold: lust (uncontrolled passionate desire), anger, and greed. These three urges should be renounced if freedom is desired. A person who (if deluded) discards the advice to be found in scriptures (is not ethical in his behavior), and is the slave of personal desires, he does not attain Self-realization, the highest goal. Therefore, let the words of the wise be the authority for determining what course of action should be taken and what should be avoided. (6-24)

Partially enlightened people intuitively sense that there is law and order in the world which issues forth from a higher sphere. Materialists tend to think of the world as a place in which to express themselves according to their personal whims. They seem to think that the world is here almost as if by accident, and that man alone should do with it as he wills, without considering the purpose for the world's manifestation. A materialistic person is concerned with the physical body and strives to make the most of his personal life in this present incarnation because there is nothing beyond it, or so he believes. We are, if we are to be free, to resist the urge to dominate others and force our selfish will on the world. Of course, anyone can change, even the most negative of persons, because even in the materialist the Light shines, but it is obscured by lack of reason and as a result of identification with matter, which has suppressed the soul's intuition.

It is suggested that a person who does not know how to behave in society turn to the scriptures and follow the rules of ethical conduct. At least this will assure order and outward harmony. Beyond this, of course, is the ability of a Self-realized person to function intuitively at all times, doing what is right moment by moment, without having to think about it and without having to order his life according to the dictates of another.

Chapter Seventeen

THE THREE KINDS OF FAITH

Arjuna continues to inquire:

What about the nature of people who neglect scriptural injunctions but who are blind in devotion and who have simple faith? (1)

Krishna explains:

The faith of people is threefold, according to their basic nature (i.e., depending upon whether they are influenced by the elevating, activating or deadening tendencies). Man (man's evolutionary status) is exactly what his believing is. Rightly resolved (but partially deluded) people worship the gods, restless (and still more deluded) people worship the spirits of demigods, and completely deluded people worship spirits of friends and relatives and ghosts. Extremely materialistic people with religious impulses, perform self-punishing austerities, injure themselves and suppress the workings of Spirit. (2-6)

We can tell by the way we worship just what our level of understanding is. If we are elevated we contemplate either Pure Being or, lacking this aptitude, the enlightened souls who are examples of the spiritual life. In this way we attune to their level of consciousness and, in time, attain their level of understanding. Those who are restless and a little more deluded, tend to think in terms of communing with intelligent (but not enlightened) entities in order to control circumstances and the environment. Here we find magicians and sorcerers. Here we also find religious "do-gooders," who are forever busy without ever knowing what, really, is the best thing to do. Then, at a lower level, we find fully deluded people with a religious impulse, whose highest idea of what constitutes a bright soul is a friend or relative who has left this world; usually they (the departed) are as unenlightened afterwards as before. And, usually, what is considered to be "contact" with such souls is self-deception or fraud (if a medium is involved). The people who are even worse off are the ones who dislike themselves to such an extent that they punish themselves and thus injure the body, weaken the mind, and become unfit for concentration and spiritual practices. Bodily weaknesses brought on by fasting, sleeplessness, extremes of any sort, sometimes result in hallucinations which are mistaken for spiritual perceptions. We should not confuse self-discipline, which is the right direction of energies and talents, with self-torture. Buddha taught: "The habitual practice of asceticism or self-mortification, which is painful, unworthy, and unprofitable, ought not to be followed." To keep the body in good condition through exercise, right diet, and the practice of cleanliness is all that is required of us, and will insure that the body is a fit instrument through which our soul capacities can be expressed when the light of intuition begins to shine.

By the foods we take into the body, and by our manner of giving, the level of understanding can be determined. Those who are on the upward way love foods which promote life, vitality, strength, health, joy and cheerfulness. Restless people are drawn to partake of foods which are bitter, sour, overly seasoned and which are hard on the system. Lower types eat tasteless, stale and unclean foods. (7-10)

Usually, we take foods in combinations. But, according to the *Gita*, by the choice of foods that we prefer, we reflect our level of consciousness and reveal our self-esteem—or lack of it. The foods we eat make up the body, so we are wise to be careful in the selection of what we eat, without giving in to fanaticism.

The Three Kinds of Faith

High-minded people give according to scriptural law, without any expectation whatever of reward. They give wisely because they feel it to be their duty to make right use of the substance of this world. Restless, selfish people give for the sake of expected reward and for the sake of personal recognition. The lower types give grudgingly, if at all, without faith, and they tend to try to get things for nothing, that is, without making just compensation.
(11-13)

God-attuned people share with an open hand and heart, so that the process of world redemption can continue. Free sharing is not a matter of indiscriminate giving; it means giving without holding back, through proper channels, where the giving will do the most good on all levels to maintain the social order and to take a truth message to people who are seeking. Restless and selfish people give only with the thought of getting something back, or because they can be publicly recognized for their participation. Even metaphysical students who give so that God will give back to them are giving for the wrong reason, according to the *Gita*. The belief that God will return our gift tenfold or a hundredfold may help us to become more trusting, but to give in this way is to give selfishly. True giving, in the highest sense, is a matter of our inwardly knowing that we are now in the full awareness of God and in need of nothing. We no longer think of giving and receiving. We distribute the resources and the available substance of nature, which have no beginning or end.

Fully deluded people pay for service (spiritual or otherwise) only if forced, and make excuses for not giving. They are supremely self-centered and think only in terms of "getting," even if others have to work to provide for them.

Discipline of the body is said to include reverence for the spiritual teacher, pure intentions, cleanliness, control of vital energies, and non-violence. Discipline of speech includes the effort to speak kindly and to be truthful. Discipline of the mind includes silence (at appropriate times), self-control, and high resolve. This is all to be observed without any expectation of reward. Whatever we do in order to gain name or fame is a waste of time and is not of lasting value. Harming ourselves or others is destructive and such behavior is due to ignorance. (14-19)

To worship God with heart, mind, and complete Being seems to be the ideal as set forth in the *Gita*, as well as all other world scriptures.

Whatever we do should be accomplished in the spirit of God. In this way we rise above the tendencies in nature and become established firmly in God-realization. Then all methods, techniques, systems and ways need never be considered again, for they are but tools and, when the goal is reached, we can lay them aside.

Chapter Eighteen

THE SUPREME RENUNCIATION

The *Gita* insists, not on renunciation of action, but on action with renunciation of personal desire. This is the true holy life. The message here is that a person can continue to render service to the world even after having attained enlightenment. A liberated person, unlike a person in bondage to the senses, is not compelled to perform action; he acts for world good and to be an instrument through, and as, which the Divine Life expresses.

In answer to Arjuna's questioning about the nature of renunciation and the relinquishment of desire, Krishna responds:

> Wise people know that true renunciation is a matter of giving up all actions which are prompted by desire; relinquishment of the results of all works is the highway to freedom. There is much confusion about this in the minds of many people. We should not give up (cease from) self-discipline and controlled (with good purpose) action, but we should work without personal attachment or desire for gain. To cease from the performance of a rightful duty is unwise and is an indication of ignorance (dullness). A person who ceases from activity because of the possibility of resulting suffering or misfortune is not the true worker (in truth). A person who does what must be done, when it needs to be done, is properly motivated. It is impossible for a person to give up action altogether because of the basic nature of a human being (with its tendencies and urges). A person who is active in this world, when he leaves it experiences pleasure, pain, or confused mental states depending upon his activity and his attitude towards it. A person who is a perfect renunciate is free upon leaving the

body because there are no subconscious impressions to influence him. (2-12)

We are, to the best of our ability, to work with an impersonal attitude, doing useful work for the good of mankind and without thought of reward in the near or distant future. In this manner we become released and no longer tread the path of cause and effect, of karma. Some truth seekers, those who live away from the world, perform only what is required for them to survive in the body. They may be rendering useful service if they meditate and strive to clear mass consciousness (by "seeing through" the sense of illusion).

Now there are five factors involved in every action: the body, the ego, the deluded soul, that (desire) which starts the action, and providence. Whatever a person undertakes to do, these five factors are involved. Because of these, if a person thinks that he alone is the doer he is mistaken. But a person who is selfless, even in the midst of action, he is eternally free, regardless of what he does. (13-14)

In every human action there are many influences which interact: the body, the sense of self (ego), the deluded soul, the vital energies which respond to the urge to act, and the unknown and unexpected chance, luck, or Divine Will which sometimes seems to intervene. The best laid plans of men sometimes go astray, for better or for worse, because of this final factor—the unpredictable—which is either the externalization of a Superior Will, or of a deeper subconscious knowing on the part of the soul, which is working for long-range good. However, we can only do the best we can in any given situation. As long as we strive to reach the highest rung on the ladder and utilize the fullest potential of which we are capable, we can do no more. The pressure of heredity and environment, even that of nature, can be overcome by the will of man when Divine guidance is present.

At a certain level we can see that some human responses are actions of nature and are not due to the soul's desire; in

The Supreme Renunciation

this way we can observe what happens to, and about, us and be free. Many philosophers feel that man is an ego and that all actions can be traced to this fact. According to the *Gita*, they err: ego is only one of the determinants of human action. The time comes for us on the spiritual path when we stand aside from the ego, the sense of separate self, and see that Universal Intelligence and Being is the Eternally Real, and that all outward activities are products of delusion taking place in the field of nature.

When we are liberated we will not do anything wrong, incorrect, or which goes against the laws of nature and society.

> The insight by which Spirit is perceived in all manifestations, undivided even while seemingly divided, this is the insight of the enlightened. Insight which reveals that different manifestations are separate and distinct is the perception of restless and unenlightened people. But a person who sees the outer manifestations as the only expression of life, without discerning the cause, that which is Changeless and Real, is dull and materialistic. (20-22)

These verses explain themselves and reflect the level of understanding of people at different stages of understanding in relationship to the life process.

> An action which is performed because it must be performed (something that needs to be done for the maintenance of society) without personal desire, attachment, or revulsion, is an action performed by a nearly enlightened person. A restless person performs action, if impelled, and with personal effort. Random action or behavior is performed by unenlightened people. (23-25)

The best way to act is freely, and with an attitude that "what must be done must be done and that is it." With no untoward reaction whatsoever does a wise person handle his responsibilities. If we feel that we are suffering as a result of being forced to act, and if we work but with a feeling that the work is disagreeable, we are not working in the highest manner. There is a difference between an act of love and an act of law, an act of grace and an act of obligation. While we renounce selfish actions we must also be aware of the effects of our actions upon others who are involved.

A person who is free from attachment, who has no evidence of egotism in his manner or speech, who is filled with zeal and who is unmoved by thoughts of success or failure, is near to enlightenment. A person who is a slave to passion (uncontrolled desire) and who eagerly seeks results from personal efforts, who is influenced by feelings of joy or sorrow, is of a restless nature. An unbalanced person who is vulgar, obstinate, deceitful, malicious, lazy, and who is forever procrastinating, is deluded. (26-28)

Here is presented a challenge to all people who would overcome their base nature and rise high in this incarnation.

There are three kinds of understanding. The first is that understanding which is controlled by discrimination and discerns what is right (in any situation) from what is undesirable. The second kind of understanding (controlled by passion) is mistaken in judgment. The third kind (the lowest) sees everything in a distorted manner. Steadiness also is of three kinds. Full self-control is highest and best, self-controlled steadiness of mind for the purpose of personal gain is second, and the lowest is when the mind is taken over, for the most part, by grief, fear, depression and sleep. Happiness, too, is of three kinds, depending upon which tendency in nature is influencing a person. The highest comes as a result of Self-realization, which puts an end to sorrow. Temporary "happiness" as a result of mere sense pursuits is the second kind, and the lowest of all is that which is derived from excessive sleep and laziness. (29-39)

Controlled attention enables us to accelerate our spiritual

progress by our ability to perceive clearly and accomplish our tasks quickly. In this way we eliminate wasted motion, we save time, and we avoid confusion. We all seek happiness in some manner. Some people seek the highest happiness, the bliss of Self-realization. Others who are restless seek temporary happiness in the pursuit of wealth, power, and glory as ends in themselves. Deluded people find a perverted state of happiness as a result of violence and antisocial acts. When we practice meditation and control the mind we give up the lower kinds of happiness for the happiness which never changes.

> No person, either on earth or in the astral and mental realms, is completely free from the tendencies throughout nature. All men are compelled to action according to which tendencies dominate their natures. Philosophers, warriors (soldiers, policemen, those whose real responsibility it is to uphold the laws of the community and country), businessmen, and laborers are distinguished, if they are in their right place in the scheme of things, according to their qualities. Serenity, self-control, austerity, purity, uprightness, wisdom, knowledge, and faith in religious practices are the natural characteristics and duties (activities) of the philosophers and sages. Heroism, vigor, dependability, resourcefulness, generosity and leadership are the characteristics of warriors. Business and trade are natural to organizational men. Working for others, rendering the best possible service, is the duty of the laborer. (40-44)

Society, as a functional organization, is dependent upon the orderly cooperation of all of its members. Therefore, all people involved should be considered socially equal in spite of the fact that individuals differ in capacities and skills. Each person, under optimum social conditions, should have the opportunity to offer his respective gift and to unfold his capacities. True democracy is not uniformity but integrated variety, where every person is responsible for his actions and is respected for his contribution. The *Gita* declares that all work, regardless of what kind it is, which contributes to the well-being of the whole is of equal value.

> By being devoted to his particular duty a person can attain spiritual perfection. We are right if we do our particular duty as best as we can, rather than try to usurp another's place and perform imperfect work. A person should not cease from useful work, if it is the best he knows (to perform), even though his situation may seem less than perfect, because all enterprises have some defects. A person who does his work in the best manner possible and who remains inwardly absorbed in the realization of his true nature, transcends outer conditions and circumstances and becomes liberated. (45-49)

A fully organized society needs philosophers and seers; it needs scientists, organizers and workers. Philosophers know the inner workings of creation because of their awakened intuition and superior powers of reason. Scientists probe into nature's secrets by using their aptitudes and skills. Organizers (businessmen and politicians, for instance) run the world by coordinating the forces revealed by men of science and the human energy of the masses. An ideal situation would be to have a flow, from the top, of wisdom put to use for the good of all men. Every "king" should have his philosophers to instruct him and give him wise counsel. Then there would be no wars and no exploitation of any person or groups. Unfortunately, the religious figures who are sometimes invited to associate with politicians and organizational leaders are not always true philosophers with universal vision.

It is quite possible, and often happens, that a person can move from one level to another, by associating with those of a higher level and by preparing himself through education and experience to handle the responsibilities of his new position.

> After a person has attained the highest perfection while in the body he can attain the Supreme Vision. With pure understanding and controlled thoughts and actions, keeping his own counsel, being moderate in all things and prac-

The Supreme Renunciation 113

ticing deep meditation, removing from his consciousness everything that is not God-like, such a person becomes purified and knows the Ultimate Truth. (50-53)

The end of human endeavor is Self-realization, regardless of the levels through which we pass. Eventually, to know Pure Consciousness we must rid ourselves of all negation, restlessness and distortions. Having done this we will find that only God exists, expressing as us.

It is impossible to fully describe this God-conscious condition. Just as we know we have a body, so we will know that we have arrived at the condition of Pure Consciousness when we do. There will be no need of evidence or proof. Any abilities that come as the result of our new insight should be accepted as natural. We should not glory over new abilities and benefits which seem to naturally come to us, if they have to do with the created worlds, physical, astral, or mental, for these will, in time, pass away.

Having become Self-realized, a person is even-minded and does not grieve (cling to things past) or desire anything. As a result of devotion a person becomes a knower of Truth and then becomes Truth. The way to freedom is to work, surrendering all to Spirit. Spirit animates all forms; we should identify with this animating Power. This teaching is the secret of secrets. A person who contemplates it fully should then follow his highest intuition in the matter of taking action in the world. (54-63)

Even while in the body, if we assume the right attitude we can live the divine life. After knowing about the facts of life we then become aware that we are Life Itself. We can say, as did Jesus and others, "I am the way, the truth and the life."

It is literally true that we are to be "saved through grace." Grace is the activity of the Holy Spirit in, and through, man which transforms and regenerates him. Man cannot perfect himself, but the movement of the Holy Spirit through him can result in perfection. If we, through egotism, feel that we can resist the ultimate purpose of Spirit, which is to liberate us and all people, we make a drastic mistake and we extend our time of suffering in this and future incarnations. We can fight against the stream which is carrying all souls to liberation but, in the end, our energies will be wasted. There is a cosmic plan at work; it is responsible for the awakening of the religious impulse in all men and it is the force that drives all men to Self-realization. Therefore, the sooner we decide to cooperate with this plan the sooner we will cease to be subject to darkness, delusion and pain. Enlightenment usually comes as a result of a series of insights, each revealing more of the truth about life than the preceding ones. Spirit is not indifferent to man's welfare, even though man does have some free choice in the matter of either cooperating with the uplifting current or resisting it for a time. We cannot miss our ultimate good, but we can temporarily resist.

We should learn to think for ourselves and discover for ourselves. We should not react to life from a basis of blind belief or false considerations. Belief should be justified through rational thinking. A true teacher inspires and instructs a student but does not compel him to accept without thinking.

Now to conclude, Krishna makes his final appeal to Arjuna:

> The soul is dear to Spirit; therefore Spirit will always instruct in a manner which is best for the seeking soul. By concentrating the attention on Reality a soul perceives Reality. By surrendering everything to Spirit a person finds release from all human troubles. This high teaching is not fit for people who are not devoted to Truth and who are cynical or disrespectful. A person who, in turn, teaches others this philosophy (or way to Self-realization) and has the highest devotion, will surely become enlightened. No one performs a more useful service than the one who teaches others the way to spiritual freedom. A person who studies this wisdom in the right light becomes free. One who hears about and believes (puts into practice what he learns) shall become god-like. Now, has your confusion, born of ignorance, been dispelled? (64-72)

The Supreme Renunciation

All that is required of us in order to know the Truth is that we empty our hearts of all that would prevent the actualization of our spiritual capacities. If we open ourselves totally, our spiritual forces will move in and through us and "make us shine like a blazing light." For a person who is weary of "trying to become spiritual," here is hope. The way is through self-abandonment, letting the inner Light reveal the way, step by step, as It most surely must.

Krishna declares that dedicated souls are the ones prescribed to teach others for, after all, we must teach according to the inner Light; otherwise, teaching will be a matter of the blind leading the blind. It is the duty, according to this scripture, for those who have been initiated on the spiritual path to initiate others. In this manner the ageless truths are passed on through the centuries. It is summed up in this verse: "May the deluded become virtuous, may the virtuous attain tranquillity, may the tranquil be freed from bondage, may those liberated ones make others free."

One thing is certain: the world needs more truth teachers to work selflessly to awaken and guide those who seek. A teacher should share from the highest vision, and the student should listen with respect and try to live the true spiritual life. He should also support the teacher or his vehicle, the organization or movement, which makes it possible for others to learn. In this way everyone cooperates and world enlightenment unfolds that much more quickly. God needs clear and willing channels through which to work out the plan of cosmic freedom.

At the end of this period of instruction Krishna, who has explained the essentials to Arjuna, inquires as to whether or not he has been successful in his efforts, and if Arjuna is now in a better condition to move forth and assume his responsibilities.

Arjuna responds:

My delusion is banished and through the grace of God I recognize the Truth. I am stable now, with my doubts removed. I shall act according to these words of wisdom. (73)

Now Arjuna, as with any who have sought a better way, can move ahead with confidence. Now he becomes an instrument through which God's will can be expressed; no higher station can be wished for by any man. Once we have been informed as to the facts of life and the wisdom of right behavior we can make an intelligent choice. Jesus taught, "I seek not my own will but the will of Him who sent me." To be able to respond to the inner urge and let the Divine will have Its way is the way to freedom. By doing this we renounce the sense of separate existence, banish egotism and experience eternal life. By shedding all pretense, excuses, false ideas and considerations, and by purifying the five coverings of the soul, we accomplish the purpose towards which we have been working for centuries.

The facts of the cosmic process are not philosophical propositions, but basic truths. Their meaning is known as we reverently contemplate them in the depths of meditation. When true vision and purposeful action are joined, for the welfare of all men, we are practicing Yoga in the highest sense. Human perfection, or what passes for that, is the result of marriage between lofty thought and ethical action. This, according to the *Gita*, must be the constant aim for one on the spiritual path.

The reader will note that, following the lofty tone of the middle chapters, the attention is again brought back to the need for man to learn to live in this present world, illumined by the Light of Lights. Therefore, the message is clear: while we are here we are to become embodiments of our soul capacities, and thus render useful service as we exhaust the motive force of unconscious drives (i.e., work out our karma and neutralize subconscious desire-patterns). In such a manner do we demonstrate what is highest and best.

In conclusion:

Wherever there is Krishna (Supreme Consciousness) and Arjuna (a devoted disciple on the path of Truth), I think, there will surely be fortune, victory, welfare and morality. (78)

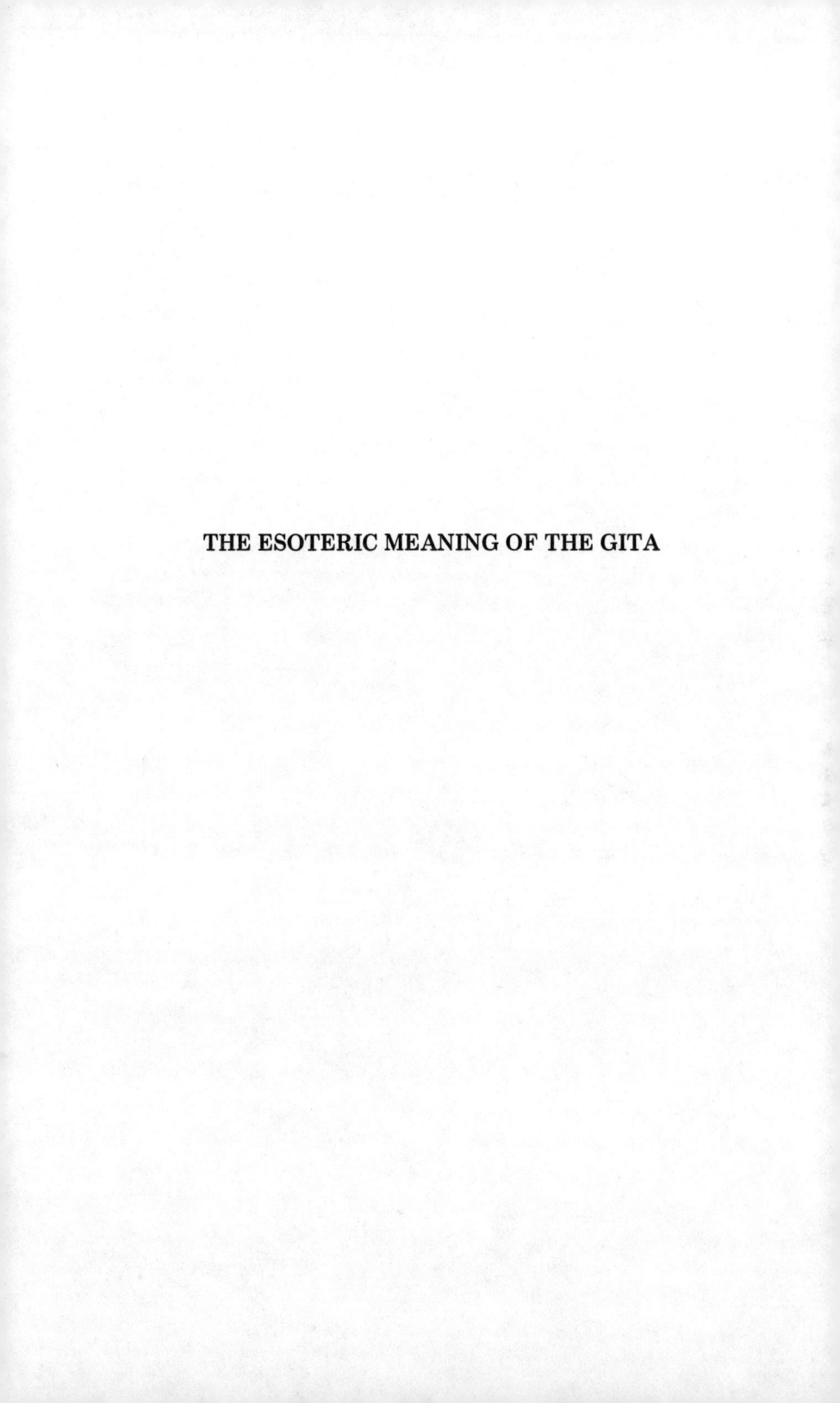

THE ESOTERIC MEANING OF THE GITA

A SPIRITUAL EXAMINATION OF THE ESOTERIC MEANING OF THE BHAGAVAD GITA

Chapters two through eighteen of the *Gita* can be better understood by the reader who possesses the metaphysical key— that the *Gita* is really a Yoga scripture designed to assist the seeker on the path to experience God-realization and liberation of consciousness. Studied simply as a guide to ideal human behavior, the scripture will still serve the reader well. However, to acquire insight into the inner meaning, one will have to understand the opening chapter; it is here that the ground is prepared for the instruction to follow.

In Sanskrit literature, the first chapter usually serves as an introduction to the total work. I have purposely reserved the material in this chapter for the last part of the book, because the majority of readers will not be scholars but persons who will want to read a popular presentation for guidance, inspiration, and for occasional help in a moment of need.

I learned from my guru, Paramahansa Yogananda, to approach the study of any scripture with the understanding that a truly inspired literary work could be interpreted on several levels. There is always an outer meaning and an inner one. There is often also an interesting story that can entertain the reader and serve to impart a moral and ethical message. Yoganandaji had, of course, studied the *Bhagavad Gita* during his years of training under Sri Yukteswar. This great master of Yoga used to conduct regular *Gita* classes, and would make notes on the scripture which he would later take to his guru, Lahiri Mahasaya, for approval and comment. It is the contention of my guru line that in order to fully comprehend the message of the *Gita* one should first have an understanding of the *Yoga Sutras*, that classic text on meditation by the sage Patanjali, as well as have a grasp of the philosophy of life and consciousness revealed in the *Vedas*.

In the narration, the opening scene is set on a battlefield, where two opposing armies have gathered. One side is made up of those who represent righteousness and the other, unrighteousness. The situation is a symbolic one. As a novel describing the conflict between opposing factions, it can be entertaining reading. As a Yoga scripture, it can be a guide to Self-mastery, because the real battle is a spiritual-psychological one, which takes place within the body, mind, and consciousness of the person who aspires to God-knowledge.

For readers who are familiar with the literal translation of chapter one, it will be extremely helpful to understand the inner symbolism, the interpretations of the names used for the various characters mentioned. Each character represents characteristics, attributes and influences of either the partially deluded mind, reinforced by ego-sense, or the aspirations, attributes and influences of the soul. The real purpose of the *Gita* is to reveal how it is possible for the aspiring soul to overcome and transcend the limitations and drives of the lower nature. Each name in the list here provided is followed by the root meaning, as well as, in most instances, a literal meaning. This is a unique aspect of the Sanskrit language: a word is made up of sound combinations which actually convey the true meaning of the word.

1. ABHIMANYU — Highmindedness. (above passion)

2. ANANTA-VIJAYA — That power that subdues eternally; spiritual qualities. (endlessly conquering)

3. ARJUNA — The purity of mind and heart, the aspiring devotee, renunciation. (the white)

4. ASVATTHAMAN — Worldliness, superficiality, love of transient things. (that which will not stand or last until tomorrow or the dawn)

5. BHIMA — Dauntlessness, control of breath; control of the

The Esoteric Meaning 121

forces of nature, endless strength. (the formidable)

6. BHISHMA — The Self appearing to be separate from God, the individual consciousness, first cause of sense of separateness. (the terrible)

7. BHURISRAVAS — Irreverence, lack of devotion. (frequent motion)

8. CHEKITANA — Higher intelligence, one who sees through the illusory fabric of nature. (intensely shining)

9. DEVADATTA — Devotion, the power to abide in the divine. (the gift of God)

10. DHRISHTADYUMNA — Self-control, leader of the spiritual forces. (intense light or splendor)

11. DHRISHTAKETU — Restraint. (intense flame)

12. DHRITARASHTRA — Father of matter side of nature, illusion, the physical form. (the firm kingdom)

13. DRAUPADI — Loyalty, the child of keen perception. Wife of the five Pandavas and daughter of Drupada. Draupadi's five sons are the controls of the five senses:

    SRUTASOMA — Renowned for spiritual knowledge.
    SRUTAKIRTI — Renowned for glory.
    SATANIKA — The hundred-formed one.
    SRUTASENA — Renowned army.
    PRATIVINDHYA — Like the Vindhya mountains.

14. DRONA — Revolution through experience in the material spheres. (vessel)

15. DRUPADA — Keen penetration, concentration, pure love. (swift-footed)

16. DURYODHANA — Passion, lower desire (hard to fight)

17. GANDIVA — Bow or bridge direct from divinity, a present given to Arjuna from Agni, the Divine Fire.

18. HANUMAN — The spiritual light, the principle of spiritual discernment, the monkey ally of Rama. (big jaw, a monkey)

19. KARNA — Selfishness, bigotry, evil desire which has become an opposition, hence a stimulus on the spiritual path. (a helm)

20. KING OF KASHI — Divine pleasure, enthusiasm, a sun-quality. (the shining)

21. KRIPA — Kindliness and pity without discrimination, emotion. (kindness)

22. KRISHNA — The Supreme Self in man, the Universal Self. (Black; the dark mystery of Truth)

23. KUNTI or PRITHA — Pandu's first wife, mother of three older Pandava brothers, spiritual intellect which is sin-destroying.

24. KUNTIBHOJA — Peace and pleasure derived from the destruction of negative tendencies. (sin-destruction-enjoyment)

25. KURUKSHETRA — The plane of human consciousness and mental activity, the field of the body. (plain of Kuru, an ancient charioteer)

26. KURUS or KAURAVAS — The blind father of the material aspects of nature, the dark forces of the universe, the undeveloped propensities expressed in man's lower nature.

The Esoteric Meaning

27. MADRI — Pandu's second wife, mother of the Pandava twins, the spiritual intellect which is compassionate. (compassion)

28. MANIPUSHPAKA — The power of an initiate in the esoteric mysteries. (a jewelled serpent or wise man)

29. NAKULA — One of the Pandava twins; the stillness of the mind. (night) The inseparable twin of Sahadeva.

30. PANCHAJANYA — That power of Krishna which extends over the five races, the five elements and the five senses.

31. PANDU — Conscience, inner knowing of divinity. (the pale, the pure)

32. PANDUS or PANDAVAS — The father of the spiritual aspects of nature, the light side of the universe, or the virtues expressed in more enlightened man.

33. PAUNDRA — That courage and valor that shatters all opposition beneath its power. (that which shatters)

34. PRINCE OF KASHI — Spiritual splendor. (light)

35. PURUJIT — Control of mind and senses. (many-conquering)

36. SAHADEVA — The other Pandava twin; spiritual awareness, devotion (always shining, day)

37. SAIVYA — Blessedness, the enlightenment that brings liberation. (blessedness)

38. SANJAYA — Reflection, introspection, turning within for guidance and understanding. (the completely victorious)

39. SATYAKI — Truth; Krishna's charioteer. (truth)

40. SAUBHADRA — Auspiciousness, happiness due to kindness. (beautiful, fortunate) One of Arjuna's wives.

41. SIKHANDIN — Illumination, halo of spirituality. (bearing a crest)

42. SOMADATTA — Inconstancy. (gift of the moon)

43. SUGHOSHA — The power of harmony. (a pleasing sound)

44. UTTAMAUJAS — Highest valor. (highest strength)

45. VIKARNA — Heresy of hatred, repulsion, dislike. (a strong helm)

46. VIRATA — Equanimity. (without attachment)

47. YUDHAMANYU — The quality of dispassion.

48. YUDHISHTHIRA — Righteousness, Dharma. (firm in battle)

49. YUYUDHANA — Truth, faith. (wishing to fight) Krishna's charioteer, also called Satyaki.

We now proceed with an examination of chapter one, with both a literal and spiritual translation and explanation.
Dhritarashtra asked:

Tell me, O Sanjaya, assembled on the holy plain of Kurukshetra, desirous to fight, what did my sons and the sons of Pandu do? (1)

Dhritarashtra is the "father of the matter side of nature, illusion, that which maintains the firmness of the kingdom." Dhritarashtra represents the individual mind which is somewhat awakened but not yet enlightened; therefore, it is blind to ultimate Truth. Unenlightened mind resorts to introspec-

The Esoteric Meaning

tion (Sanjaya) in order to acquire a degree of insight and understanding. The verse can be read: "Unenlightened mind inquired through the process of introspection: assembled on this holy plain of Kurukshetra (the body of man), what did the tendencies and drives of lower mind (my sons) and the virtuous inclinations of the soul (the sons of Pandu) do?" That is, "What happened; what was the outcome of the struggle?"

In the original Sanskrit text the first two words of the first verse are: "Dharmakshetra-Kurukshetra." Dharmakshetra refers to the field of righteousness and Kurukshetra refers to the field of unrighteousness: the inclinations within the mind and body of man which tend to draw the soul's awareness into the confusion of the material realm. While the outer battle is one between two armies which represent virtue versus nonvirtue, the real inner battle for one on the spiritual path is between the tendencies and drives of ego-dominated unenlightened mind versus the influences of the soul in the direction of total freedom and knowledge.

The embodied soul functions through the nervous system, mind and body. When the nervous system and mental field are refined and cleansed of restrictions, the soul can express freely through the body and live totally in harmony with the forces of nature, including a harmonious relationship with the uplifting force in nature *(dharma)* which maintains balance and encourages evolutionary unfoldment.

A yogi who meditates experiences a play of consciousness in the brain, spinal pathway and body. Within the subtle body of man (the fine electric (astral) body which interpenetrates the physical form) are channels through which life-force *(prana)* circulates. Nerve force, a grosser aspect of prana, circulates throughout the nervous system, allowing consciousness to pervade the body. There are distribution centers for nerve force and there are distribution centers through which prana moves. These latter distribution points are known as *chakras*; it is at the chakras that life-force changes in frequency to perform various functions in the body.

When soul force and consciousness descend into the body

with sufficient intensity, almost all attention is carried through the senses into contact with the outer world. Therefore, one in this condition is almost totally "worldly" relative to interests and inclinations. When consciousness functions, for the most part, through the three lower chakras, a person is primarily concerned with material needs, emotions, sensations and the perpetuation of ego-needs. When consciousness moves through the higher chakras, the inclination of the person is to seek out the real purpose of life and to live a more God-conscious existence. Dharmakshetra, the field of righteousness, has its base in the crown chakra in the brain. Kurukshetra, the field of the body, has its base at the lowest chakra, with forces playing through it and the two above it.

The chakras are seven in number. The crown chakra is in the mid-brain (and above it) and is often represented in paintings of saints as a halo or light above the head. The spiritual eye is located at the point behind the space between the eyebrows and is the positive pole of the *medulla oblongata*, at the base of the brain. It is from this point that both prana and nerve force are directed downward into the body. The cervical chakra is located in the spine, at the neck; the dorsal chakra, in the spine opposite the heart and lungs; the lumbar, in the spine opposite the mid-section and solar plexus; the sacral, in the spine at the small of the back. The coccygeal chakra, at the bottom of the spine. Considering the five lower chakras in relationship to states of consciousness, the lumbar chakra is midway between the lower and higher points. This chakra, then, represents Arjuna's level of awareness as he begins his ascent to the realization of Supreme Consciousness—which is related to the crown chakra.

> The Prince Duryodhana, having seen the Pandava forces arrayed for war, approached the teacher, Drona, and spoke these words: Behold, O teacher of the sons of Pandu, this mighty army arrayed by the son of Drupada, thy gifted pupil. In this mighty army stand heroes who are great archers and equal in battle to Bhima and Arjuna. Here are the invincible Yuyudhana, Virata, and Drupada; Dhrishta-

The Esoteric Meaning

ketu, Chekitana, and the valiant King of Kashi; Purujit, Kuntibhoja, and Shaibya, the greatest of men; the powerful Yudhamanyu, and the brave Uttamaujas, the son of Saubhadra, and the sons of Draupadi, all lords of great chariots. (2-6)

By understanding the inner meaning of each name we can begin to comprehend what is taking place. Duryodhana (passion and lower desire which fights hard and is difficult to master) turns to the teacher, Drona (change and revolution through experience in the material spheres), and describes the various forces and influences gathered for the contest. The first named are the attributes and influences of the soul. These include Yuyudhana (truth, faith), Virata (equanimity), Drupada (concentration, pure love), Dhrishtaketu (restraint), Chekitana (higher intelligence), the King of Kashi (enthusiasm), Purujit (mind and sense control), Kuntibhoja (peace and pleasure as a result of overcoming negative influences), Shaibya (positive discipline), Yudhamanyu (dispassion), and Uttamaujas (highest valor) the offspring of Saubhadra (happiness due to kindness). These represent the positive qualities, the virtues which contribute to enlightenment and righteousness.

Hear me again, O best of the twice-born, while I tell of those who are distinguished among ourselves, the commanders of my army. These will I name to thee, that thou mayest know them well. Thyself and Bhishma, and Karna and Kripa, the victorious in war; Asvatthaman, Vikarna, and Jayadratha, the son of Somadatta. And gathered here are also other heroes, well skilled in battle and armed with various kinds of weapons, determined to lay down their lives for my sake. Unlimited is our army, commanded by Bhishma, whereas that army of the Pandavas, defended by Bhima, is insignificant. Therefore, being stationed in their proper places in the divisions of the army, let all support Bhishma alone. (7-11)

Now the aspects and tendencies of the forces of unrighteousness are named: the teacher, Drona (change and revolution through experience in the material world, memory and habit), Bhishma (ego-sense), Karna (selfishness), Kripa (kindness but without reason, emotional sympathy), Asvattahaman (desire),Vikarna (hatred, dislike), Jayadratha (body-bound inclination), offspring of Somadatta (inconstancy). Also referred to are the "other heroes," who are well skilled in battle, i.e., the many tendencies and drives produced from those already mentioned.

And true to one who is deluded, passion and desire interfere with intuition and reason and cause one to declare: "The army commanded by the ego-sense is unlimited, whereas that army made up of the forces of virtue, defended by Bhima (control of the forces of nature, endless strength) is insignificant. Therefore, let us order our ranks and support the cause of ego-sense alone."

> At this point, to encourage the heart of Duryodhana, Bhishma, the eldest of the Kurus, the powerful grandsire, roared like a lion and blew his conch. Thereupon, conches, kettledrums, tabors, trumpets and cow-horns all together blared forth suddenly from the Kaurava side. The noise was tumultuous. (12-13)

To encourage Duryodhana (passion and desire), Bhishma (ego-sense) used available vital forces in the body to stir desire for sense experience, resulting in inner turmoil, false excitement and confusion. When unenlightened mind's desire is strong, it resists the soul's natural inclination to seek peace and inner self-completeness.

> Then stationed in their great chariot, yoked to white horses, Krishna and Arjuna blew their celestial conches; Krishna blew his Pancajanya and Arjuna his Devadatta, and Bhima of terrific deeds and enormous appetite blew his mighty conch. Paundra, Prince of Yudhishthira, the son of Kunti, blew his Anantavijaya and Nakula and Sahadeva

The Esoteric Meaning

blew their Sughosha and Manipushpaka. And the King of Kashi, the Chief of the archers, Sikhandin, the great warrior, Dhrishtadyumna and Virata and the invincible Satyaki; Drupada and the sons of Draupadi, O Lord of earth; and the strong-armed son of Saubhadra, on all sides blew their respective conches. The tumultuous uproar resounding through the earth and sky rent the hearts of Dhritarashtra's sons. (14-19)

When the clamor of the ego-driven senses becomes powerful, there awakens in the true devotee the soul forces which result in an upward flow of creative energy from the base chakra. This flow stimulates the vital forces related to each chakra and one hears inner astral sounds. Soul force draws the devotee's attention back to the source of Life within the body, back to the crown chakra, the field of righteousness.

The reference to white horses indicates purity and the influence of *sattva guna*, which is influential in upholding the way of virtue. The superior influence of inner celestial sounds weakens and neutralizes the inclinations of the senses. Hence: "The tumultuous uproar resounding through the earth and sky rent the hearts of Dhritarashtra's sons (all of the inclinations stemming from passion and desire)."

Especially during deep meditation, one may inwardly hear the various frequencies of vital force active in the chakras: from the base chakra, the sound of a frantic bumblebee; from the sacral chakra, the sound of a flute; from the lumbar chakra, the sound of a harp; from the dorsal chakra, the sound of a pealing bell; from the cervical chakra, the sound of a mixture of frequency-influences; at the spiritual eye, the sound of OM, the Word, the Primal Sound. Listening to these sounds and being absorbed in them, one can easily flow from material consciousness to transcendental awareness. By following the inner sound back to its source, one's attention is almost effortlessly led to the experience of the Absolute, the non-dual Reality.

Then Arjuna, whose banner bore the crest of Hanuman, looked at the sons of Dhritarashtra drawn up in battle order; and as the flight of missiles (almost) started, he took up his bow. And, O Lord of earth, he spoke this word to Hrishikesha (Krishna in his aspect of lord of the senses): Draw up my chariot, O Achyuta (Krishna in his aspect of the unchanging one), between the two armies, so that I may observe these men standing eager for battle, with whom I have to contend in this strife of war. I wish to look at those who are assembled here, ready to fight and eager to achieve in battle what is dear to the evil-minded son of Dhritarashtra. (20-23)

Arjuna's banner bore the crest of Hanuman, which symbolizes eventual mastery over mental restlessness. One on the spiritual path must overcome the tendencies which cause mental restlessness if he is to attain higher states of awareness during meditation. It is also well for one, early on the spiritual path, to engage in self-examination in order to clearly identify the existence of influences of both higher and lower natures, which have to be handled and utilized. Arjuna declares his desire to "look at those" tendencies, habits, drives and influences which are inclined in the direction of fulfilling the desires and appetites of the unenlightened mind, driven by ego-sense.
Sanjaya revealed:

Thus commanded by Gudakesha (Arjuna), O Bharata, Hrishikesha drove the most magnificent chariot and placed it between the two armies facing Bhishma, Drona, and all the rulers of the earth. Then he spoke: Behold, O Partha (son of Pritha), all these Kurus gathered together. There saw Partha, in both the armies, fathers, grandfathers, teachers, uncles, brothers, cousins, sons, grandsons, fathers-in-law, comrades and other friends, all arrayed for war. Then he, the son of Kunti, seeing all his kinsmen drawn up in battle array, was overwhelmed with deep compassion and thus spoke in great sorrow: (24-27)

Hrishikesha (Krishna) is represented as driving Arjuna's chariot. That is, he governs the five senses while, at the same

The Esoteric Meaning

time, is impartial and aloof. In the *Gita* narration Krishna has chosen an objective stance, taking the side of neither army. While he can instruct, it is up to the participants, especially Arjuna, to decide upon a course of action. Partha (Arjuna) observed, in both the armies, the family of tendencies and influences of both factions. When he sympathized with the conditionings, habits and memories of his lower nature, which had been accumulated over many years of experience, he was reluctant to destroy them. They were part of his personality; how could one remove that which has contributed to his present psychological condition?

Arjuna said:

> O Krishna, as I see my own kinsmen gathered here determined to fight, my limbs fail me, my mouth is parched, I tremble all over and my hair stands on end. The bow Gandiva slips from my hand and my skin burns. O Keshava (Krishna), neither can I stand upright. My mind is in a whirl, and I see adverse omens. Nor, O Krishna, do I see any good in slaughtering these, my own people, in battle. I desire not victory, nor sovereignty, nor even pleasure. (28-31)

At times, when confronting the seeming awesome challenge of overcoming undesirable and destructive tendencies, even though the final goal is glimpsed, one is overcome with reluctance to even begin the confrontation. Habits and tendencies of the individual can be the result of experience or of learning; that is, we might acquire certain conditionings as a result of living life the best we can, or we might acquire them through association with others. We might even inherit some tendencies from our parents. It does not matter how the undesirable conditionings have been acquired; what is needed is for one to decide to remove the undesirable characteristics so that the desirable ones might be dominant. There is another problem, also: one might not be able to imagine how future pleasure and earthly happiness is possible without the existence of patterns and habits which have been part of past pleasant experiences. One new on the path does not fully realize that the supreme pleasure is that which results from Self-realization. After enlightenment one can experience life in this or any realm in total freedom.

Arjuna's bow represents his ability to enter into battle. He is so overcome with indecision and sorrow that his bow slips from his hand, indicating his temporary inability and reluctance to face the challenge before him. He states, in effect: "I do not want victory or mastery. I do not even see any purpose in entering into the process of transformation."

Arjuna continues:

> O Govinda (Krishna), of what avail is dominion to us; of what avail are enjoyment and pleasure, or even life itself, if these for whose sake we desire kingdom, enjoyment and pleasure, teachers, fathers, sons, grandfathers, uncles, fathers-in-law, grandsons, brothers-in-law, and other relatives, are gathered here to fight, giving up all hopes of life and wealth? O Madhusudana (Krishna), even if they were to slay me, I could not kill them, not even to gain dominion over all the three worlds, and how much less for the possession of the earth! What satisfaction could be ours, O Janardana (Krishna), in killing these sons of Dhritarashtra? Sin alone would take possession of us in slaying even these felons. Therefore, Madhava (Krishna), how could we be happy in killing our own kinsmen? (32-37)

Arjuna is still under the spell of deluded pity and, therefore, does not speak with wisdom. One would have to be unwise to ask: "What satisfaction could be ours in doing away with the tendencies of the unenlightened mind, driven by ego-sense?"

Arjuna continues:

> Although these, with understanding overpowered by greed, see no evil resulting from extinction of families, and no sin in hostility to friends, why should we not turn away from this sin, O Janardana (Krishna), since we clearly see the

evil due to the destruction of the family? From annihilation of the family comes the destruction of its immemorial religious rites. And when its spirituality is destroyed, the whole family is doomed to unrighteousness. O Krishna, when unrighteousness overpowers a family, its women become corrupt; and when women are corrupted, O Varshneya (Krishna), intermingling of the castes is sure to arise. Intermingling of castes leads the destroyers of the family and the family to hell. Their ancestors fall, being deprived of offerings of food and water (ritual offerings). By such caste-confusing misdeeds of the destroyers of the family, the immemorial religious rites of caste and family are destroyed. Thus we have heard, O Janardana (Krishna), that the abode of hell is inevitable for men whose family rites are destroyed. Alas! What a great sin we are about to commit, having resolved to slay our kinsmen, actuated by greed of the pleasures of the kingdom. Better indeed, would it be for me, if the sons of Dhritarashtra, weapons in hand, should slay me in battle, while I remain unresisting and unarmed. (38-46)

Arjuna declares that since the forces influenced by ego-sense and unenlightened mind "with understanding overpowered by greed" see nothing wrong with maintaining their position, why not avoid the conflict, since we (he and Krishna) know better? As the narration continues we encounter a double message, one for social instruction, another for spiritual education.

Arjuna observes that, until now, virtuous inclinations and ego-caused tendencies have, after a fashion, lived in harmony. This is how it is with the person who is considered to be normal in society; he learns to live with his psychological condition, neither truly happy nor really unhappy, neither enjoying heaven nor experiencing hell. But if the arrangement is changed, there may be chaos and destruction of the known personality condition.

When change is introduced, if transformation is not orderly, there is the possibility of disruption. Things will never again be as they once were. One may even think in terms of negative and destructive tendencies becoming dominant, resulting in the suppression of spiritual impulses, so that the "whole family" is doomed to a life of unrighteousness. When the feminine (feeling) nature is corrupted, then disorder is the rule in one's life. In some cultures, still, people are encouraged to honor departed relatives (as well as the "gods", the forces of nature) in order to maintain communication with the subtle planes and to contribute to an orderly relationship among all factions and influences.

But what if the ego-sense, with its tendencies and influences, is not honored and it falls? What will become of us then? What if the divine nature can no longer influence us? What will be the outcome of that unfortunate event? Arjuna is attempting to understand the process of transformation from the perspective of mixed feelings and unclear understanding. His intuition is not yet sufficiently awakened. Although he is duty-bound to face his challenge, he shrinks from it. Perhaps he is thinking, "If the forces of ego-sense and unenlightened mind win the battle, I will simply be unconscious and will know nothing of it—so perhaps it would be better to give up before I begin?" This attitude is reflected in the final verse:

Sanjaya said:

Thus speaking in the midst of the battlefield, casting aside his bow and arrows, Arjuna sank down on the seat of his chariot, his mind overwhelmed with grief. (47)

In this verse it is stated that Arjuna actually cast his weapons aside. Earlier, they had slipped from his hand. Now he has decided to avoid the confrontation.

Even this phase, that of temporary despondency, can be useful to one on the spiritual path, because it can be the opportunity to examine what is really important in life. Many people live out their lives with a minimum of self-examination and never actualize even a fraction of their full potential. They come to terms with inner and outer circumstances and adapt, rather than aspire unto the heights which are possible

The Esoteric Meaning

of attainment. It can be after an episode such as this, an episode of honest self-analysis, that one is prepared to enter into a program of study and practice in order to fulfill his true purpose for having come into the world.

Chapter one concludes:

> *In the Upanishad of the Bhagavad Gita, the science of the Absolute, the scripture of Yoga and the dialogue between Sri Krishna and Arjuna, this is the first chapter entitled The Despondency of Arjuna.*

When the philosophical basis upon which the *Bhagavad Gita* rests is understood, the full meaning of the scripture is better comprehended. Chapter one sets the stage for what is to unfold, while chapter two imparts the philosophy and purpose of the text. In the original Sanskrit version, chapter two is entitled, *Samkhya Theory and Yoga Practice*. Samkhya refers to one of the six major philosophical systems of India, and the word itself refers to the enumeration, or numbering, of stages and aspects of Universal Consciousness, from the Absolute to full manifestation as the processes of nature. This system of thought was expounded by a teacher known as Kapila and teaches that knowledge of an object is possible only when knowledge of its components is experienced. Twenty-five categories are taught as the basis of creation and the cosmic evolutionary process. Further, it is emphasized that it is possible for a person to acquire direct insight into the nature of Reality by examining and experiencing all levels of consciousness, from the material plane to the most subtle, and from the most subtle to the Absolute. A brief examination of these twenty-five categories follows:

1. *The Unmanifest Field* — The Absolute, Transcendental, Reality which is beyond even the most subtle level of creation. The Source of all manifestation and the Realm of all knowledge. The creative process and the knowledge of it can never cease to be, because the Unmanifest Field is stable and

permanent, without beginning or end. It is unbounded Pure Existence.

2. *Initial Manifest Substance and Consciousness* — The field of God, the Larger True Self of every soul. Here are found the gunas, the attributes and influences which make possible manifestation. Here, too, is Spirit involved with nature, or God.

3. *Movement in the Direction of Manifestation* — Due to an urge within the Godhead, the gunas or attributes become agitated and mixed, resulting in the production of the universe, from subtle to gross. When the equilibrium of the three gunas is disturbed, the forces of nature interact to produce the worlds and to send forth specialized units of Consciousness to ensoul forms.

4. *Individualization and Involvement of Consciousness* — The manifesting substance which makes possible creation has four components. They are: light particles, time, space, and the original creative force. The intelligence of the creative force directs the creative process. Spirit (Consciousness) here identifies with the creative process and life is evident, expressing through various life forms. This is the stage where units of Consciousness assume a degree of a sense of separation from the Source. What is termed ego-sense, in this philosophical system, appears at this stage.

5. *Cosmic Mind* — An omnipresent creative field. There is but one Mind; the seeming individual minds are but portions of it. The soul working through mind is referred to as "man." The Sanskrit word, *manas*, also means "thinking principle."

6-15. *Ten Principles Connecting Mind with the Manifest World* — These provide the basis for the five senses of perception and the five organs of action. Senses include hearing, feeling (touch), sight, smell, and taste. Organs of action include speech, motion, excretion, generation, and manual skill.

The Esoteric Meaning

16-20. *The Essences of the Objects of Perception* — These express themselves as the five elements which go to make up the objects of the senses and provide the basis for the material universe. The essence of sound expresses itself in space, the essence of touch expresses itself in air, the essence of sight expresses itself in fire, the essence of taste expresses itself in water, the essence of smell expresses itself in earth.

21-25. *The Five Elements Making Up Material Creation* — These are designated as earth, water, fire, air (gaseous substance) and ether (fine matter).

According to this philosophical view, all that is manifesting in the outer realms has a common origin and a common reality. This is why it is said that there is but one substance, one Life and one Reality in, as, and through the worlds.

Center for Spiritual Awareness has world headquarters in northeast Georgia. *Here on a ten-acre site are found the spacious education building, administrative offices, residence homes, library and meditation temple. CSA is not a commune, nor is it a spiritual community in the usually accepted sense. It is a service center from which literature and training aids flow to a waiting world, and a retreat center to which seekers come for instruction and spiritual refreshment.*

If you would like informative literature about books, recordings and available programs, you have but to contact the CSA office. There is no obligation. We are here to serve you as you unfold your inborn divine potential. Contact: Center for Spiritual Awareness, Lake Rabun Road, Post Office Box 7, Lakemont, Georgia 30552.